PARENTING
for *Life*

MADELEINE STANIMEROS

To Mum and Dad
for teaching me to fly

PARENTING FOR LIFE

Written by Madeleine Stanimeros
Edited by Jo Neil
Designed by Ella Leighton

ISBN 978-1-5272-2529-9

Published by Lionheart Publishers UK
First published, 2018

Printed by Beamreach Printing
Cheshire, WA13 0JB

CONTENTS

FOREWORD

We met the Stanimeros family soon after we arrived in Cheltenham over ten years ago and Mads has become a close and treasured friend.

Like many, we have been welcomed into their usually bustling home frequently and always warmly. Whether it is making friendships at the school gate, throwing a party for a child or a grown-up, mentoring a teenage lodger or spoiling friends or family with her fabulous cuisine, Mads has a genuine heart for each one.

There is so much that marks Mads out... her love and compassion for others, her discretion with sensitive issues, her insight into the unobvious and her keen observation of the ridiculous. Her laugh and sense of fun is second to none!

It does not take long to discover that Mads' passion is for children and families. Over the years she has developed her skills and been able to share her expertise through magazine articles and blogs, running parenting courses, offering parents one-to-one coaching and delivering school presentations to parents on the benefits and pitfalls of social media use in the young.

This book is an inspiring look at some of the ways we can become the best parents we can for our children and at how we can navigate some of the inevitable challenges involved, never losing sight of the need to enjoy family life to the full.

- Jane Pringle (mother and family doctor)

INTRODUCTION

I remember bringing our first child home and the heartfelt wishes I had for my tender, innocent baby as he snuggled contentedly in my arms.
In my naivety, I hoped I would never get cross with him and neither we, nor life, would ever bruise him.

Now I have journeyed a little further (and had four more), I realise that wishing all those things for him would have been lovely if he were always to remain a baby. However, the tools needed to be a responsible adult require a little adversity and parental courage, particularly amid the challenges of the current climate.

Today's children face earlier academic expectations, exposure to an over-sexualised world and more online pressures than ever before, resulting in reports that evidence the decline in self-worth and mental wellbeing of many young people. Parents can be understandably fearful about the negative influences and burdens on their children and wonder how to help and protect them. Be reassured, we are not powerless.

We can ensure that their main influence is from us, not from the world around them. It is possible to establish good values in the hearts of emotionally-secure children and protect them from the cultural tide. We can help them to self-regulate in their world of many choices.

I don't believe there is such thing as a parenting expert so I don't claim to be one. But I am privileged to support parents who want to grow in their role, as well as those who have challenges (don't we all?). This is through hosting courses, speaking at events and conferences or in private consultation. I love to share ways of helping children to grow in character without crushing them or the parent/child relationship. I am always encouraged to hear the stories of parents after they've successfully tried something I've shared.

As we've journeyed through parenting over the last 23 years, we have found and developed a handful of valuable concepts that I wish had been handed to us as we carried our first child home. These are the ones I want to hand on to you.

HOW TO USE THIS BOOK

Growing a family can be a little like growing a garden; the hands-on, muddy-booted, sleeves-up, messy job of gardening is a good metaphorical description of the exhausting, exhilarating and rewarding privilege of parenting.

Throughout this book I have used gardening analogies, inspired by gardening enthusiasts I have visited across England. Some have small plots and others have extensive grounds, but all have known the battles and victories of establishing something beautiful, in spite of the many challenges.

The book is divided into two sections: Soft Love and Strong Love, which describe different approaches to parenting. Soft Love explores how to connect and build emotional trust with our children, whilst Strong Love has tools to help our children to develop wisdom and responsibility.

To help you to establish your own family culture, I've included a few pages throughout the book on different values you might want to bring into the home. There are many different values to consider as you ponder your long term vision for your family. Each value has the power to affect the feeling and atmosphere in your home, so each one begins *"The power of…"*

Additional, specific information is given about how our brains work, which helps to explain some of our children's choices and behaviours.

Some tools are light-hearted, others are more gritty. You can enjoy snippets or read it all from start to finish.

"We will be parenting adults far longer than we will be parenting children."
– Tim Grew, pastor, father of four (young adults)

PLANTING

I remember an experiment from my school days where we grew two sets of seeds; one in the dark and one in the light. Surprisingly, the plants in the dark began to grow taller than their counterparts. But later, after their exponential growth, they failed to thrive and some even died.

Whilst they were striving upwards towards the light, they were not putting down the necessary root system to sustain them later. This seems a fitting analogy for the concerns of today's parents who are conscious of the dazzling lights of the world alluring their children to fast-track growth with promises of freedom.

We all hope our children's lives will be filled with adventure and fun. We're also conscious that for them to get the most out of life, establish healthy relationships, and grow to be all that they can be, they need some solid foundations as well as core strength to resist the not-so-healthy temptations of the world around them.

Soft Love

HOPES AND DREAMS

BELONGING

UNDERSTANDING FEELINGS

CHOICES

DIFFERENT WAYS TO LOVE

The Bridge

Our children need us to be strong, but they also need us to be soft. Nobody can build security and confidence into a child more than their own parents. Some Soft Love is second nature to a parent, but there is also so much to learn that is not instinctive. The tools in Soft Love can help us to connect with our children in a way that will build a lasting trust.

Imagine a beautiful bridge. The most beautiful bridge you can think of. For some of you that might be a little humpback bridge in a Japanese garden over a lily pond with wild orchids growing up the side, and for others that might be a grand piece of engineering, like Clifton Suspension Bridge; almost impossible, yet stable and impressive. Imagine this bridge is co-owned by you and your child and it represents your relationship. You own one half and they own the other. In order to cross freely and safely at all times, both of you need to keep your side of the bridge in tact.

When each child is very small, you can model how you keep your side clear and show them how to look after their side. This includes showing them how to avoid weeds setting in and rubbish accumulating or rust taking hold and small cracks causing larger ones and making it unsafe to cross. As they grow older, you can begin to draw backwards and trust them to start to tend their half, inch by inch, until they are fully tending their own side of the relationship.

If you keep your side clean and clear, free of rot and rust and decay, then one day you'll be able to say that, no matter what your differences with your child, no matter what choices your children have made, what alarming, embarrassing or disappointing things they (or you!) might have done, it's always safe to cross.

CHAPTER ONE – HOPES AND DREAMS

Landscaping

Just over 32 years ago, John and Ros Wallinger bought a home, near Hartney Wintney in Hampshire. The garden was nothing more than an unkempt jungle. What they didn't realise when they bought the property, Upton Grey, was that underneath the jungle were the foundations of a very special garden designed by the esteemed hauticulturalist, Gertrude Jekyll.

Every plot of land, whether stately, humble, large or tiny, is rich with potential. It is a blank canvas for the owner to envision possibilities, whether that's a lawn for children to play, a place to grow fruit and vegetables, somewhere to open to the public or just a place to sit with friends. The owner would also be wise to consider the hidden riches in its soil, foundations or aspect, in order to bring it to its full potential.

Our role as parents is to envision the family we would like to grow, the culture we would like to set and the values we would like to sow into our children. But it's also ours to discover what is already within them. John and Ros saw the wilderness that stared back at them and they imagined beauty, but they were not gardeners. They needed clues about what lay in their jungle and they needed a vision and a plan.

Parents are visionaries

What sort of family do you want to grow? What kind of adults do you hope your children will become? Some people have already thought deeply about their vision for their family and you may well have too. However, for others it's an enlightening concept – it certainly was for us.

Parents often feel empowered when they realise that they can be proactive in parenting, not just reacting as issues arise. They look out to far reaching areas of life – way beyond the bitty needs of today – and find they have a vision for the culture of their family and strong hopes for the characters of their children, not just now, but into their adulthood. After all, we will be parenting adults for a lot longer than we will be parenting children, so if we want to reap a good harvest, we need to plan what we sow.

> Sow a thought, reap an action;
> Sow an action, reap a habit;
> Sow a habit, reap a character;
> Sow a character, reap a destiny
> - Stephen R. Covey

Planning begins with having some dreams and making decisions now which will impact tomorrow. Some of these dreams may be small, like saving for something or losing some weight, others may be large, such as a career aspiration or a specific hope for your child's future. Moving them from dreams to hopes is the first step towards reaching them – like a ship sets the coordinates it's heading for: if it's sailing to Africa but starts its journey one metre off-course, it won't be long before it is miles off-course and headed for Brazil!

Most of us are used to planning for practical reasons, whether that's a party or a holiday, but it usually starts with a pen and paper (or the tech equivalent!). Many of our friends have built extensions and not one of them has broken ground before spending hours completing a set of plans exact to the last centimetre. Yet we can navigate our parenting without a sense of direction and a plan. Some of you are natural planners and this will appeal to you. Others are wingers and you might be backing away slowly, uncomfortable with the idea of planning when you just prefer to evolve. Take heart!

This is not a way of deciding what careers our children have or tailoring their personalities. It's just identifying your family priorities so that they don't get buried under the busyness of every day.

Lack of planning doesn't mean we won't achieve anything good, but it does limit our potential.

"Without vision, people perish." – Biblical proverb

If we've established our priorities, we're less likely to get distracted by the daily issues and choices that come our way. Or by the choices that other parents are making, or even choices that others might be implying that don't line up with our own! We can either be like a well-rooted tree that stands its ground when the wind whips up, or we can be blown all over the garden. In order to bed-in our priorites, it can be helpful to ask ourselves questions to establish what our own vision is for our family.

Here are a few good questions to ponder:

- How would you like people to describe your family?
- What sort of adults do you want your children to become?
- How do you want your children to respond to challenges?
- What kind of relationships do you hope you'll have with your adult children?
- What sort of friendships do you hope they'll have with each other?
- What do you feel is a good balance of work, rest and play?
- What do you hope your children will contribute to the world around them?
- What habits don't you want your children to have?
- How do you want to be remembered as a parent?

You might not have directly thought of those questions before, but chances are you'll have some ideas about the answers you'd give. Those answers will be part of your vision for your family. Life will always throw us some curves, but if you've got a vision, you're more likely to stay on course through the distractions.

As we began working in our own wilderness that came with our house, we encountered all sorts of assailants that threw us off course: frost, foxes, bindweed and even the sun can cause havoc. However, with a clear sense of direction, you can get back on course.

In spite of all the neglect in our garden, the well-rooted trees, which had been lovingly tended as saplings, survived beautifully and they produce an abundance of fruit to this day.

At the end of this chapter there is a list of more questions you can ask yourselves as parents. As you answer, you'll begin to see your vision evolve. From there you can decide on which habits to develop yourself and with your children (and which ones not to bother with!). This can be open-ended as you progress through family life.

As parents, each of you is a work in progress. We had no idea how to garden when we bought our patch. In just the same way, nobody comes to parenting as a finished product, ready to hand on their expertise on life to their children. Quite the contrary – we grow as they grow.

It's worth saying, at this point, that there is a difference between a goal and a vision. A goal has a finite point of accomplishment, for example, to learn to tie your shoe laces or pass an exam, but a vision has a longer perspective – possibly even an infinite one. Whilst raising children we will have lots of goals for them, but our vision is about the longer perspective; the sort of adults we hope they will become... which in turn will influence others and on it goes.

Let's go through four sample questions and look at what some visions might be and the possible steps towards them. We'll look at some small specific visions and some big abstract ones:

"A well-rooted tree laughs at the storms." – Malay proverb

WHAT DO WE WANT TO BE REMEMBERED FOR?

This will differ from family to family. We wanted our children to feel "Mum and Dad really understand me." We didn't want our kids to have secret lives away from parents who "just didn't get us." So an overarching aim for us was to really accept and understand them.

For this we've had to develop the sometimes all-consuming habit of listening well. In fact, we had to *'learn'* how to listen well (sadly it's not an innate human skill). Stopping, prioritising, learning how to empathise, hearing their perspectives (even when we didn't agree with them), putting time aside to spend with each child, were habits we made time for and honed (and we're still learning!).

VISION: That our children felt really understood and accepted, so they could trust and share with us through highs and lows, through awkwardness and embarrassment, as young children, teenagers and then adults.

PLAN: To learn to listen well; to read books on effective listening; to accept their perspectives and feelings; to put intentional time aside for each child; to create an emotionally-safe environment.

WHAT SORT OF RELATIONSHIPS DO I WANT MY CHILDREN TO HAVE WITH EACH OTHER?

A family from one of my courses shared this:
"I didn't think I needed a plan to know that I wanted all my kids to build good friendships with each other. But the questionnaire made me realise that we weren't being proactive about it. Often the kids just passed in the hallway and extracurricular activities meant that we were rarely all at one meal. We decided to make a plan; to put things in the diary that gelled us together. We made time to gather and share things about our lives – our challenges and victories, both practical and personal. Because we were intentional, other things were turned down in order to uphold the decision we'd made to spend time together. At times that was hard."

VISION: For our children to form good, lasting relationships within the family.

PLAN: Prioritise family times. Plan family walks, games and meals; make times where mobile phones and other distractions are laid down; normalise deeper questions; practice listening to each other; model and encourage how to share life's issues appropriately with each other.

"We noticed that the children began to take a greater interest in the detail of each other's lives, asking each other about difficulties they were having. Sharing ideas and encouraging each other was in better proportion to competing and putting each other down."

HOW DO I, AS A FATHER, WANT TO INVEST IN MY DAUGHTER/S?

A father is an essential influence on his daughter's identity as a strong woman. Being proactive in this area will affect her relationships and the way she sees herself.

VISION: For his daughter to be confident in herself as a woman.

PLAN: Continually affirming her for who she is; going clothes shopping with her; spending time listening to her as she grows and changes; understanding her; encouraging her to establish healthy boundaries. The same question could be asked of each parent for each gender.

HOW MUCH DO WE WANT OUR KIDS TO BE INVOLVED IN THE UPKEEP OF THE HOME?

This is a good example of how a long-term vision affects the choices of each day.

I know of many parents who lament poor teenage input in the home. When they're small it's so much easier to do the work than involve the little ones. But if your long term vision is that they'll go out into the world with some domestic skills, with an attitude of participation, you may consider it's worth the extra time when they're small. At first it's like poking smoke uphill with a sharp stick, but it does pay off in the end! If the vision is in place, the small consistencies of every day contribute to that bigger picture.

VISION: For our children to take responsibility for our home and for the homes they will live in.

PLAN: Setting achievable goals; making time to encourage them to a good (age-appropriate) standard; affirming them for their contribution.

Don't let the urgent hijack the important

Looking ahead made us realise that we had lots of things we envisioned. For example, I wanted our home to be a fun place to live.

Sometimes I had to remember that vision when I was taking myself too seriously! Those are a few ideas to give you a sense of how a plan can influence your child's course and future skills. It's important that the aims and benchmarks feel right for you. It's inspiring to be positively influenced by friends or family, but unhealthy if we're reacting to what we feel others think we should be doing, or if we're intimidated by other people's standards.

You don't need to map out your week to the smallest detail, but if you have a clear vision of your priorities it will affect your daily decisions.

Nothing's perfect

Of course, there will be some successes without planning. I'm not suggesting that everything would have been a disaster. You could build an extension without any plans and have some success, but a vision will avoid unnecessary disappointment.

You can still be spontaneous! Planning doesn't mean we can't wing things a bit. In fact, once you've got your priorities in place, it's much easier to wing it because you'll be confident the important things are covered. There will be disruptions and distractions. Even people with a clear sense of destination go off track, but at least there is a track, so when they've drifted they know where to return to.

We will go wrong from time to time. I so often meet parents who carry regret or guilt. We need to give ourselves permission to go wrong. We're a work in progress.

Prioritising comes at a cost. There is always something we could otherwise be doing with our time and resources:

- Eating healthily is more time consuming than fast food.
- Listening well and encouraging sibling relationships takes patience and time.

Looking back, it's easy to believe that there wouldn't have been time for many of these things. But when they're priorities, they get preferential treatment. And the best laid plans evolve as you evolve...

I had dreams of a pretty flowerbed in our garden, but our wilderness has been tamed to a lawn, which is perceived by our boys to be a football pitch. One day I'll have my flowers!

Perfection isn't a goal, it's a trap

Questions

These questions can be considered all at once or sporadically. It's helpful to write your answers down so that you can come back to them and see if your aims and hopes line up with your practices and habits, or whether you feel the need to re-evaluate.

Choose a few questions that interest you and form an answer sheet with the visions and plans you can sow in to your life.

For every question, consider your family vision and the plans you could put in place.

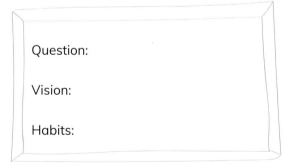

Question:

Vision:

Habits:

OUR LEGACY

- How do we want to be remembered as parents?
- How do I want to be remembered independently as a mum/dad?

OUR RELATIONSHIPS

- How do we want to treat each other and speak to each other?
- How do we want to speak about others?
- How should family members resolve issues?
- What kind of relationships do we hope our children will have with us and with each other – now and in the future?

OUR FAMILY

- How would we like people to describe our family?
- Which family do we admire and why?
- What are our highest values?

OUR HOME

- What feeling do we want visitors to experience in our home?
- How can we ensure our home feels like a living place, rather than just a base?
- What balance of work, rest and play do we want to establish?

OUR CHARACTERS

- What sort of adults do we want our children to become?
- What sort of friend do we hope they'll be?
- What level of emotional intelligence do we hope for?
- What level of confidence are we striving for in their own identity?
- How do we want them to manage stress?
- What would we like the family to appreciate?

PARENTING STYLE

- How do we want to discipline our children?
- What did we like about the way we were parented?

OUR COMMUNITY

- What sort of a neighbour do we want to be?
- How do we contribute to the community/ world both socially and economically?
- How do we hope they will view people of different races, religions or circumstances?

These are the main categories to stimulate your thoughts. They're not exhaustive. You can add to these questions with your own. You may want to consider diet, fitness, money management, talent development and home skills.

DISLIKES

Some people might also like to consider what they don't like:

- How don't we want our children to behave?
- What habits don't we like in children? Adults?
- What aspects didn't we like about the way we were parented?
- What habits and practices do we want to avoid as a family?

"Striving for excellence motivates you; striving for perfection is demoralising."

- Dr Harriet Braiker

The Power of Values

I remember the day I decided I would no longer compare myself to other mums. This meant ceasing to apologise for the state of my house or behaviour of my children (unless they'd directly upset someone). My resolution was soon put to the test.

We had trained one of our children out of nappies during a backpacking adventure. It made sense not to travel with a potty, but instead to use disposable plastic cups. Soon after we returned from our travels, a friend popped by for a cuppa, to catch up on our adventures. As she settled at the table, our now toilet-trained toddler showcased his new skill. He came running in from the garden, grabbed a coffee mug from beside the sink and to my friend's horror, pushed the front of his trousers down and had a wee in the mug. He then opened the dishwasher, threw the wee to the back of the machine, placed the mug carefully upside down on the shelf, closed the dishwasher, washed his hands, then ran outside again.

My friend's jaw was on the floor. Against all my instincts, I remembered my recent resolution not to defend myself, kept calm and carried on. "So, how have you been?" I asked.

She pulled her jaw off the floor and gently asked, "Why doesn't he pee straight into the machine?" Good question! As tempting as it was to feel like a very poor role model in comparison to other mothers, who surely wouldn't tolerate this behavior, I let it go.

- Who's the best parent?
- The most patient?
- The most laid back?
- The most kind?
- The most organised?
- The best cook?
- Who's never compared themselves to anyone else?

FREEDOM
Here are three great ways to cut yourself free from those defensive moments.

CELEBRATE OTHER PEOPLE'S SUCCESSES
As parents we can affirm others, rather than check our progress by them.

NOTICE WHAT YOU HAVE ACHIEVED AND WHAT YOU FEEL GRATEFUL FOR
Start with the smallest things. Gratitude changes our whole outlook.

DON'T DEFEND THE STATE OF YOUR HOME OR YOUR CHILDREN
Live by your own values, not the perceived values of others.
We're wired to be all that we can be as parents, but it gets muddled when we define ourselves (or our children) by external benchmarks. If we're okay with the way we are, we're far easier to be around.

"Comparison is a thief of joy." - Theodore Roosevelt

CHAPTER TWO – BELONGING

Choosing the Right Soil

Different gardeners will put different combinations of plants together to get the effect they are looking for. But some things are designed to belong in certain settings.

When I was ambling through Morag Dobbin's garden with her in the pretty Cotswold village of Winchcombe, she pointed out a willow tree that had been mistakenly planted on a mound some years ago. She said, "That willow doesn't belong there and it looks out of place. Willows are most often found in wet situations, on riverbanks and in low-lying places because they thrive on a lot of water."

She explained that it should have been taken to a place where it belonged when it was still small, but it's too big to transplant now.

Our children are designed to belong in our family and they will intuitively know that, but intentionally developing a strong sense of belonging gives them security. If they're not bedded in securely they can look for other places to belong.

Belonging? Well, you might well wonder what on earth this is doing in here! Whatever feelings you had when you brought your first baby home (recently, or years ago), you probably didn't doubt for a second that they belonged in your family.

But belonging and having a sense of belonging are two different things. One is a fact and the other is a feeling. For example, you might be in a sports team because you've made the standard. But to feel like you're accepted as a key part of the group is a whole different issue. That depends on your ongoing experiences with the coach and other members of the team – whether they make you feel like you're one of them.

It's the same in families. You can know that you belong, but certain experiences can give you the feeling that you are a significant member of the group. These experiences deepen your children's roots in your family which, in turn, strengthen your children's security and self-worth.

A child's emotional well-being is deeply impacted by the feeling that they have a place in the world where they belong.

As much as we want our children to belong in all sorts of places, clubs, teams and friendship groups, we also know that they might only pass through those places. It's also possible that they will experience exclusion as well as inclusion there. In order to develop security there needs to be a place where they feel their belonging is an unconditional, constant certainty. Home is a great place for that.

Creating belonging at home doesn't just give children comfort and security, it's a basic need. Psychologists list belonging as one of our top psychological needs.

Inclusion

SO HOW DO WE CREATE A SENSE OF BELONGING?

There will be many things we already do instinctively that give our children that sense, but there are also things we can intentionally do to reinforce their sense of belonging.

When I was invited to speak on the topic of belonging, I asked some of my advisors (my own children) the following question: What is the difference between being in a family and being part of a family?

One of them replied:
"To be part of something, you have to contribute as well as receive." How true. Did you know that savvy politicians and business-leaders have worked out that if they want someone's allegiance, they don't shower them with gifts, they ask them for a favour? That makes them feel important. Clever!

Being able to contribute makes you feel valued. It sends the message that you're needed in this group. How would you feel if the affable Jamie Oliver tracked you down and said, "I've heard about a certain recipe of yours and would love to share it in my new book."? Pretty pukka, I'm guessing! Inspired to follow? That might be a bit far-fetched, but there's something to be gleaned here: our children look up to us. If they grow up knowing that their contributions are valuable to us, their self-esteem will soar.

Inviting their opinion (even when you don't need it) gives their esteem a boost. It helps them to develop awareness in situations, rather than just tagging along. It also sends the message their

perspective is valuable. Remember, lots of little experiences often send a stronger message than one big experience. When they're small we don't have to do all the thinking. We could ask:

- *"Shall we stop at the shop on the way or the way back?"*
- *"Do you think the red one or the green one looks better on me?"*
- *"Which cake should we make when friends come around on Thursday?"*
- *"Which flowers do you think we should plant?"*

That might all sound a bit obvious, but when days are busy and we're in 'get on with it' mode, it's not always instinctive to ask their opinion.

As they get older, we can invite them into our challenges (appropriately, of course). Tell them a little something that went wrong in your day and ask them what they would have done. I'm often amazed by their insights.

Share something you've seen in the news and ask what they think about it. Let them know a challenge that's ahead, and ask them for advice.

" Our interests, motivation, health and happiness are inextricably tied to the feeling that we belong to a greater community with common interests and aspirations."

- Gregory Walton, psychologist

Another inclusive family idea is to do something as a team that benefits people outside the family group. Here are some ideas:

Finding a charity to support together gives them a sense of 'team'. Tiny donations from birthday money or pocket money soon add up. Posting or wiring the money you've all contributed, is immensely satisfying for them. It doesn't have to be bank-breaking, it's the principle that matters:

- One family chose to make a sandwich each time they went to town and gave it to a homeless person. Another brought sweets to keep in mum's bag for the same purpose.
- A local family helped in an elderly neighbour's garden together.

Creating a strong sense of belonging in the family will give them a place where...

- they feel safe to express ideas, preferences and needs:
- they learn to strive for the values of the group, not just for their own ideals.
- they don't feel excluded when their opinions are different or when they get things wrong.
- their personal identity and self-assurance are boosted.
- they can enhance their abilities and learn to relate well to others.
- they can attain a sense of belonging.

'Belonging' is one of the key attractions of social media. A strong sense of belonging at home will strengthen them for when they explore online.

So whilst belonging is technically a birthright, it's amazing how many advantages there are to *sensing* belonging as well as just *knowing* it.

Cohesion

One way to strengthen family bonds is by having family meetings. Meetings sound a bit formal, don't they? They needn't be, they can be as much fun as you make them. We call ours Family Circle, but you could come up with a far more creative name than that.

It's just a set time where you can regularly talk about events or issues, share encouragements, ask questions and make plans. If your children are very small, you could store this idea for a couple of years, but it's worth bearing in mind that they can contribute from a very young age and that starting whilst they're young means it will always feel a natural part of family life.

"If you want your children to keep their feet on the ground, put some responsibility on their shoulders." - Abigail Van Buren, columnist

You can choose the goals of your meetings and allow the children to shape it over time. Having a treat at the meeting goes down well. We have hot chocolates with all the toppings (it lures them in!). Agreeing on the rules of play is helpful, for example, everyone gets a chance to talk, nobody interrupts, other people's ideas do not get laughed at or put down. You can have a little book to write down the things you've discussed, especially if some goals have been set.

Sometimes it helps to ask some questions at the beginning to get them engaged, for example:
- What's one thing you're grateful for this week?
- What's a personal goal you'd like to set or have achieved?
- What's something you're hoping for?

The main part of the meeting could contain all sorts of things. Here are just a few ideas to give you a framework:
- Discuss what to do at the weekend or where to go on holiday. Research and agree on a new game to buy.
- Think about a family boundary that someone wants to challenge or set. This could be based on a frustration (what state we leave the bathroom in, was one of mine). One of

our children is still proud of challenging the 'no chewing gum' boundary. It's one of my irrational aversions. It was debated and agreed that they can chew all they like on Sunday afternoons.
- Chat about the earlier ideas of helping in the community, whether that's visiting an elderly person in the community, or leaving a cupcake for the postman or refuse collectors.
- Consider some ethical issues, such as plastic usage or recycling.

We had a season where we looked at family values in our meetings. We found we all valued very different things. We made a mutual set of values to uphold.

It's great to end by affirming how much you appreciate their participation and ideas. And most important of all – end on time.

Families have reported back so many advantages to the family meetings, such as a greater respect for each other, children feeling a sense of ownership around some of the boundaries, an increased sense of loyalty. Parents have noticed that the youngest or quietest child benefits from being listened to and appreciated, as so often in family life they can get spoken above and overruled by the older or bolder siblings.

"It's hard to feel you belong if your ideas aren't accepted." - A child

Traditions

Another way to create a strong family identity is through traditions. Many families will have some instinctive traditions or routines around bath-time, bed-time, birthdays and Christmas. But in this section we'll look at some extra ways to introduce traditions.

If you bring to mind any organisation or group that has a strong identity, they will have traditions. Brownies and Cubs have songs and formalities. Even countries have their customs. Finland has wife-carrying championships and the Greeks have a tradition for when a child loses a tooth. When one of our children lost a tooth in Greece one year, they were carefully nursing it to put under their pillow when an ageing aunt promptly hurled it onto a nearby roof, according to custom.

Even religions have practices for coming-of-age and marriage, and skateboarders have a particular style of clothing. All these traditions give the group, country, organisation or place a personal identity. Their members gain a sense of belonging by following their traditions.

I find when I speak on this topic it seems to unleash a plethora of creative ideas from parents.

Families put their ideas into practice and report an increased sense of feeling unique. I especially love hearing how the children have responded, both at the time as well as some years later.

Children's memories of traditions usually begin: "Mum always used to..., my dad always..., we always..., our family..."

A tradition can be big or small and work with any number, even if there are only two of you.

Examples

Here are some examples from clients, friends and children who have shared their traditions with me.

BIRTHDAY LETTER

My husband and I write a letter to give each of our children on their birthday. We tell them the things we remember about the year, the ways in which we're proud of them, funny moments and we affirm where they've shown character. When I was cleaning my son's bedroom recently I found his letters. They're dog eared and ragged, they've been read over and over.

I've shared this during a talk a few times and know that some parents do it creatively, some lightly, some with more depth. Recently one mum fed back that her child's eyes are wide with anticipation on her birthday. She loves the gifts, she loves the fuss, but she's looking out for 'The Letter'.

SHOW & TELL

We have Show & Tell every Friday as a part of family night. We take it in turns to introduce each other. In that time we show something we've made or share something we've done or seen. Everyone else has to be quiet and listen. When we've done or said our piece, the rest of the family can raise hands to ask a question.
We can show something we've made from Lego, a funny story or a picture or something new we have bought. Mum and Dad do terrible card tricks and once they announced that Mum was pregnant again.

The mum added – "I cherish the look on the child's face, whose turn it is, as they scan and decide whose hand to pick first at question time. Oh, the power!"

SATURDAY PANCAKES

We have pancakes every Saturday, made by Dad. He doesn't ration the Nutella! We even have them when we're away. We've had pancakes in fields, up a mountain and by a river. Saturday wouldn't be the same without pancakes.

BREAKFAST TREAT

Once a month Dad would take one of us out for breakfast. There are six of us, so our turn only came around twice a year. It was such a treat.

SPECIAL CHAIR

My mum would wake early on our birthdays and gather flowers and foliage from the garden and hedges. She would weave this all over the chair at the head of the table; The Birthday Chair. It always looked stunning and made you feel special to be sitting there. It was so affirming to have so much effort spent on me. Such a simple idea, but such a precious memory.

SPECIAL TIME

On Wednesday nights we took it in turns to stay up quarter of an hour later with mum. I don't know if it was the actual quarter of an hour, or just feeling special on that night that made it so good, but we loved it when it was our turn and loved that everyone else had to go to bed.

NEW SHOES

We have a terrible song that we sing when someone gets new shoes. It's really just the words 'new shoes' to the tune of *Amazing Grace*. It's so cringy, but it has to be done! As we got older and began to buy our own clothes we'd scuff our shoes so they didn't look new, but our little brother had a keen eye for something new. He'd point and say 'new shoes' and the out-of-tune family-choir would all begin... Hands over your ears and just get through it.

SHARED DREAMS

We had a large jar on the window sill and every time we had something that we were hoping for, or a prayer, we would write it on a scrap of paper and put it in the jar. At the end of the year we would tip out the jar and see how many of our hopes had been fulfilled. There was so much to be thankful for.

YEAR-END CELEBRATION

At the end of the summer term we have a BBQ and the children can bring three friends each. As the years go by it feels like the real closure to the school year and the beginning of the holidays.

POP'S SPAGHETTI

Grandpa had spaghetti night on Sunday evenings. He covered the furniture with sheets and all the grandchildren would come.

CAMP OUT

Once a year we'd all sleep on the trampoline, including the dog! I was a baby when we started, so I don't remember my first one. Now my brothers and sisters have all got older they don't join us any more, but Mum and I still love it. We need loads of duvets and blankets and a hot water bottle – and the dog.

GRATITUDE

At tea time we take it in turns to share the best thing about our day. The children love it. It's a time where we get to share and listen. Our little one loves it when it's her turn and she goes on and on! I think it makes her feel really significant when we all sit and listen to her.

Picnics in unusual places, wild swimming, family night, a cake on one day of the week, a secret family handshake, an annual round of crazy golf... Traditions, whether big or small, can leave a long and lasting sense of identity and even carry on for generations.

Traditions are a way of celebrating who you are

IN A NUTSHELL
BELONGING

- Knowing you belong and feeling you belong are different experiences
- Our happiness is inextricably tied to our sense of belonging
- Shared family experiences deepen our children's sense of belonging
- To feel included you need to feel your contribution is valued
- Invite your children into your decisions
- Find joint experiences to be part of together
- Meet as a family and engender respect by giving everyone their say and validating their contribution
- Create traditions
- Create your own unique family culture

The Power of Trust

Emotional safety might not reel off the tongue when we're asked what's most important to us, yet relationship can't be built without it. The behaviour of parents will influence whether their children think people can be trusted. The trust of our children is precious, yet it can be easily damaged by one of the following:

WHITE LIES

There's no such thing as a white lie. It's too easy to lie and get out of events or appointments; to lie about the biscuits running out, when it's just that we don't want them to have another; or lie to their teachers or school about absences or work they haven't done. If we lie, we can't be totally surprised if they don't trust us or they think little (or big) indiscretions are acceptable. By the same token, following through on promises builds trust too, even when they're very small. For example: "I'll get you a new one," or "We'll do that next week." Keeping our word to, for, and in front of our children will enable them to trust our word.

PROTECTION

Not standing up for them in front of others can break trust. Urging them to greet other adults with a hug or kiss when they don't want to, undermines their trust in our protection of them. Sharing stories about them for amusement when we haven't had their permission (either in person or on social media), can make them feel fearful and isolated, as does openly sharing our disappointments about them, for example: "She never listens!" or "He's so difficult."

They can feel vulnerable when they're disciplined in front of people too. Sometimes it's necessary to sort out a dispute with those involved, but when they've made poor choices and they're dealt with in public, it can lead them to feel ashamed.

Minimising their issues can erode their trust in us. One of our children asked me recently what an upcoming vaccination was going to feel like. If I mislead him by playing it down, he would question my honesty. If we're reliable, our children will let us stand with them through their challenges. By the same token, exaggeration

is equally confusing for them. Words like 'You always', 'You never', 'Everyone' or 'Nobody' can bring shame on them and lead them to retreat emotionally. Children sometimes do this when they don't feel safe. Emotional safety can only exist where there is trust.

COMPARISON
Comparing them to their siblings, or your experience of being their age, can cause resentment. Being accepted and understood is one of their greatest needs. Every child's experience is unique; offsetting them against a better example is shaming.

TRUTH
Our children will ask those awkward questions. In fact, we are finding our younger children are asking the big questions earlier and earlier. They do need truth from us, and simply answering the question, rather than giving them the whole context, works very well. However, there are times when they ask things they're not ready for. Since it's never helpful to lie ("You arrived by stork!") or overexpose them, ("Uncle Peter is having an affair"). It can also be helpful to delay. The author Corrie Ten Boon shares this story about when she asked her father, a watchmaker, a specific question about sex:

He turned to look at me, as he always did when answering a question, but to my surprise he said nothing. At last he stood up, lifted his traveling case and set it on the floor. "Will you carry it off the train, Corrie?" he said.

I stood up and tugged at it. It was crammed with the watches and spare parts he had purchased that morning. "It's too heavy," I said.

"Yes," he said, "and it would be a pretty poor father who would ask his little girl to carry such a load. It's the same way, Corrie, with knowledge. Some knowledge is too heavy for children. When you are older and stronger, you can bear it. For now, you must trust me to carry it for you."

As I work with parents to help their children to self-regulate in the area of social media, I find the biggest ingredient needed between parent and child is trust.

Trust can take years to build and seconds to destroy

CHAPTER THREE – UNDERSTANDING FEELINGS

Mess

I remember, when I was a child, turning over a log in our garden to find an ugly mess of insects, fungus and moss. I quickly rolled it back into place and moved away before those scampering mini-beasts could come anywhere near me. I wanted them to be washed away with the garden hose.

I later learned about the vital significance of that creepy, messy microhabitat. The germination, moisture, shelter and carbon storage under and within wood debris has global implications for our ecosystem.

Our children's feelings are messy. They usually emerge at inconvenient times and feel as though they are going to scamper all over everything. It's tempting to want them to keep them at bay, but processing feelings is vital to their emotional health which, in turn, affects their whole personal ecosystem.

Our deepest hopes

Most parents hope to have an open, connected relationship with their children when they're youngsters, teens and right into adulthood. (Was that one of your hopes when you looked at the questions in the opening chapter?) Yet we know from statistics that so many children and teenagers are struggling with emotions and will often say they don't feel their parents understand their feelings. If we can learn responses to our children's struggles that make them feel understood, they are more likely to share with us both now and in the future.

About ten years ago I had a horrible accident. I vaulted over the handlebars of my bicycle and landed on my face. My upper lip needed reconstruction and I lost my front teeth. (Sorry if you're a bit queasy, the story does have a happy, well-reconstructed ending). I remember sitting in A&E, waiting for the doctor, when a nurse came and began asking me about my cycling safety habits and advising me on protective wear. My wound was bleeding, my teeth were missing and I was vomiting from shock, yet she felt this was the moment to preach on preventative habits. I was traumatised and not ready for forward planning.

That was a real emergency. But for young, developing brains many difficulties can feel extreme. Responding with well-meaning advice when they're having a struggle, can feel frustrating for them. There will be a time for advice, but the brain is simply not ready for it until the emotional distress has been met – whether they've hurt their toe, lost a conker or fallen out with a friend.

It's tempting when our children have difficulties of any kind (hopefully not as severe as the above example), for us to get out our bucket of good advice. After all, we've got loads! We've banked so many more experiences; we itch to fast-track them to good solutions. But advice is not their first need. It might jog them on, they may even take it. But if it's doled out before empathy, they will learn to keep their feelings safe – deep inside.

I was chatting recently with a mum and her teenage daughter and I asked the daughter how she was feeling about leaving school to move on to Uni. "I'm nervous," she said. Just as I was about to acknowledge that it's a big step, her mum cut in, "You'll make some friends and you'll be fine." The daughter's face clouded over, she withdrew from the conversation. Her mother, in all her loving optimism, had just shut her down.

It's natural to want to save them from pain. When challenges arise we can so easily try to clean up the muddle with a metaphorical spray of the hose. The feelings might even look as though they've gone away, but they haven't. They're just hiding. Not long ago, I was standing next to a father and son. The little boy said that he was cold. The dad told him to jump on the spot and that he needed to be tougher. The little boy went quiet. It's easy to shut them down, even when we don't mean to:

Child: "I'm hungry."
Parent: "You can't be, you've just had breakfast."

Child: "My feet hurt."
Parent: "You just want to be carried."

Instinctive responses

Take a moment to consider what your instinctive responses might be to the following:

What would you say to your:
- Four-year-old who's spilled water all over a painting they've spent ages on?
- Eight-year-old who is frustrated because they can't find a certain, special pencil they want to write with?
- Ten-year-old who was told they are ugly at school?
- Twelve-year-old who's worried because they've left the homework questions at school (again!)?
- Fourteen-year-old who has left their phone on the bus?
- Seventeen-year-old who had worked hard toward a joint project with a friend, to be finished together this Saturday, but the friend has just cancelled?

When I ask these questions during a seminar, the responses are all similar. Here are a few of them:

- Reassure the four-year-old that they can paint another lovely picture.
- Offer alternative pencils to the eight-year-old and let them know you're sure that their favourite one will turn up.
- Tell the ten-year-old they're beautiful!
- Chat to the twelve-year-old about being more responsible and suggest they call a friend for the homework questions.
- Phone the bus company!
- Console your seventeen-year-old that their part of the work wasn't a waste of time and that it could be used for a future project.

"The solutions we find to our problems as children are the strengths we have as adults."
- Simon Sinek, visionary

All these responses are fair in their way.

Along with:

- Never mind!
- What you need to do is this...
- Come on, worse things happen!
- They probably didn't mean it!
- Don't worry, you'll be fine!

Or even:

- I can't believe you've done that!
- I did warn you...
- What???!!!
- Not again!

As caring parents, we're trying to move them on to a better mindset. It's also possible we're juggling mealtimes, school runs, extra-curricular activities, homework and trying to keep sane.

But, by swiftly solving their problems, we might not be listening. The flood on their painting might have seemed disastrous to them, perhaps that particular pencil felt important, your opinion on their appearance might not feel as significant as that of their peers. It's possible they mind enormously about the implications of their friend cancelling Saturday.

Maybe it doesn't feel fine!

As we achieve that leap from challenge to solution, we step over something vital – their feelings! Their messy, inconvenient and possibly time-consuming feelings.

Empathy

What happens when we don't take time to empathise? The problem is that if emotions are tidied up or washed away, their removal can imbalance a child's micro-climate because the pain has nowhere to be processed.

Helen's seven-year-old son is prone to anger. Recently he'd felt rejected by a friend at school. Helen explained that she'd helped her son by telling him, "Children can be hurtful, they change who they're playing with." She reassured him that his friend would play with him another day and suggested that he played with lots of different people. A few days later he exploded in a fit of anger and it turned out that her helpful advice hadn't helped at all. The pain hadn't gone away, in spite of her best efforts. It had banked up and exploded.

If issues are unresolved, children can become needy and be prone to emotional outbursts, they can also get angry and use even physical violence. They're playing out their frustration and may be developing a habit.

Another way children and teenagers deal with pain (and adults too) is to self-soothe: food, alcohol, self-harming and drugs all have the ability to numb pain. More recently they have gained easy access to a silent, pernicious and alarmingly pervasive way to dull pain: social media. When a child or teenager isn't permitted to work out their feelings without judgment or hasn't been taught how to articulate them, those feelings don't go away. They either find an expression for them in frustration or anger or try to self-soothe.

As parents, we can be influential here by lifting up the proverbial log to take a look at the mess. If we can empathise in the first instance instead of advising, pacifying, consoling or compensating, our children will feel safe to share their feelings. It's here that we can affirm their frustration or pain and help them to articulate and process those feelings.

Empathy is sitting next to them in their muddle, listening to their feelings and connecting with their experience. This validates the emotions that are bubbling up in them – even if the experience would have had a different affect on us.

Empathy is the most potent, powerful, life-changing, first response we can offer into any challenges our children have, big or small. It's the key to emotional intelligence.

Empathy is not changing someone's perspective, it is accepting their perspective

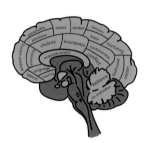

RESPONSE OR REACTION?

Have you ever wondered why your children sometimes react unreasonably to situations? Dare I say even dramatically or defensively? Here's why...

The human brain has two different regions from which to respond to challenging situations; the Amygdala and the PreFrontal Cortex.

The Amygdala is a reactor. It's that part that enables you to make choices outside the bandwidth of your normal character, such as jumping out of the window if the house is on fire. It reacts to fear and can save your life, but it can get you into all sorts of trouble because it's also the part that is responsible for people overreacting, lashing out verbally or physically.

The PreFrontal Cortex is a responder; it uses rationale and reason. It's the part that will consider options, think about potential outcomes before jumping in. It's not so useful when a speedy response is required, like when someone's trying to steal your bag. But it is the part we should be engaging for most scenarios in life to avoid overreaction.

The Amygdala develops around the age of two. This is why a toddler is able to react dramatically when another child wants their toy. The PreFrontal Cortex, however, takes around 25 years to develop (perhaps it never does for some!). This is why, throughout childhood and all through the teen years, we so often see our children's reactions coming from the Amygdala, rather than the PreFrontal Cortex.

The Amygdala will give a helpful adrenaline boost when in fear of danger. However, sometimes it works outside its job remit and responds not just to fear of danger, but all fear. Fear of:

- having its pride knocked
- being offended
- not getting what it wants
- people's opinions
- failure, loss...

You might have noticed some Amygdaline (my word) reactions from your children. Perhaps they've stomped off or said rude things or shouted (or is that just mine?). Maybe they've overreacted to you or been physical with a sibling. Many teenagers would confess to 'amygdaline' reactions on social media that they've later regretted.

As parents, we can help our children feel emotionally safe so that their issues pass from the fight or flight reactions of the Amygdala and move up to the PreFrontal Cortex where rationale and reason reign. One way to do this is to understand and empathise with their emotions.

Healing

A group of teenagers were recently asked whether they felt able to share their problems with their parents. They all answered 'no'. Here are some reasons they gave:

- *"When I have a problem like falling out with a friend, Mum will say, 'Why don't you just do xyz?' It's not always that easy."*
- *"Sometimes I just say what my parents want to hear so I'm not judged."*

Do you have friends whose first instinct is to tell you what to do or minimise your issue instead of listening to how you feel? You soon learn who to share with, don't you?

Enduring rewards come from parking those well-meaning responses and looking at a situation through another person's eyes and seeing how it looks and what it feels like to them. This sends the message, "You're upset and I want to understand." Empathy heals; it is a superpower.

Once heard and understood, children will feel safe to explore their options. Empathy involves:

HEARING

Hearing
Emotional acceptance
Articulating emotions
Listening to their responses

In order to hear our children's challenges we need to hold our fabulous advice (or exasperation) and just let them say what the problem is. It sounds easy, but let's face it, 'just hearing' when they've left their phone on the bus is pretty stretching stuff!

EMOTIONAL ACCEPTANCE

Expressing our understanding brings their heart rate back down. "This must be hard for you." "That must have been so difficult." They are not always the first words that come to my mind when my children report something alarming, but they are powerful. We become safe to approach rather than someone to defend themselves from.

Accepting our child's feelings is courageous, because you're choosing not to control that moment (that's why it's counter-intuitive!) That metaphorical bridge that represents our relationship with them is safe to cross when we accept their feelings.

It doesn't mean you're in agreement with their choices. It doesn't mean that they won't have to find solutions and it doesn't mean that you would feel the same in their situation. It just means you've understood how serious it feels to them. This acceptance takes away their need to 'act out' for your understanding. Shouting, stomping, banging doors, crying loudly, sulking, disengaging or any form of angry, defiant, uncooperative behaviour can often be a result of not feeling heard and understood. Can you remember ever shouting because your point was not understood?

ARTICULATING EMOTIONS

If they are able to, children may share the emotion they're feeling. If they don't, you could try guessing, for example, "That sounds worrying, hurtful, annoying, sad, painful..." This gives them permission to feel. It conveys that we accept those feelings and sends the message, "I get you", "It's okay to feel that way." Once their feelings are permitted they may correct your guess, "I'm not cross, I'm just really sad." Responding like this also builds their emotional vocabulary so they can learn to easily express their feelings.

LISTENING TO THEIR RESPONSE

Having their emotions heard, accepted and validated helps our children feel emotionally safe. It enables the problem to move from the fight or flight area of their brain (Amygdala) to the PreFrontal Cortex where reason and rationale reign. Then they are more likely to consider their options and possible outcomes. They may not do it immediately, they might need to process first, but they will feel free to do so. Even very small children will come up with their own solutions when they have felt heard and accepted. Their solutions are so often better than the ones we might have come up with.

When they're ready they will feel able to share their plan with you. It's so important at this point to affirm them for coming up with solutions. Your last challenge is to try not to dive in and change the plan. If you have concerns about their solution, it's better to ask questions so that they can keep moving along their rational path. Your questions can lead them to considering the outcomes of their solutions:

- *"How do you think your friend will respond?"*
- *"When do you think it's best to do this?"*

There's a world of difference between involved and interfering

Good fruit

I'm amazed, time and time again, how often small children, tweens, teenagers and young adults will solve problems once they've been heard and understood. They may well come up with the very solution that you could have come up with straight away, but the point is you've built trust and they've learned that they are able to resolve issues for themselves. They may even invite your advice at this point. But they'll be ready to hear it, unlike after my bike accident... timing is crucial.

Hearing about our children's feelings, failures, concerns and fears is not as tidy as a quick fix. It takes courage to move away from how we feel and what we want to do about it towards the uncertain world of how they're feeling about it and what they choose to do. Leaving space for them to move through their feelings before beginning to solve the problem will require your patience and time. Authentic relationship is time consuming. But every little issue they have is a powerful moment to connect with our children; a moment where they build trust for those days to come, when the issues will be bigger.

Does that mean we never advise, reprimand, shape nor grow our children? No, not at all. That's all a necessary part of parenting. This is just the simple, but counterintuitive pause where we learn to empathise as our first response.

Will they drown in self-pity? Empathy isn't a pity party. Neither is it a method of control that will bounce them out of their difficulty. It's a little time for connection that nourishes the soul and liberates them to progress. They may need time to process before they move on, but they are far less likely to get stuck if they've been understood. If they do choose to stay in their pain, we can begin to make suggestions once we have given them some time and understanding.

With a metaphorical spray of the hose we can clean up the muddle of our children's emotions. But feelings don't go away just because we're not allowed to have them, they get buried and have to find less healthy ways to get dealt with. And sadly, over time, if we solve, advise and reprimand in their challenging moments when they just need to be heard and understood, they can begin to 'tune out' our voices.

If you feel that you've reached a point where your voice has become white noise to your child, don't lose heart. Each time you choose an empathetic response you will be repairing your bridge one inch at a time. It's a slow process as trust is not built in a day, but an inch in the right direction is better than a mile in the wrong one. Life will deal us highs and lows. If our children haven't learned to process their emotions through the

"You're planting seeds that will produce fruit one day - even if it's a while before you see it." - Hils Grew, speaker, mother of four

smaller issues, they may find that grief and loss become crippling. They may develop anger and find unhealthy ways to numb the pain of their unresolved emotions.

If you can listen empathetically when your:
- Four-year-old doesn't want a bath.
- Six-year-old doesn't want to go to school.
- Seven-year-old doesn't want to get dressed.
- Nine-year-old is having a pre-pubescent, hormonal moment.
- Thirteen-year-old wants to stay out later or have more access to social media.
- Fifteen-year-old has been upset by a teacher.
- Eighteen-year-old feels rejected by a friend.
- Nineteen-year-old calls from the airport because she's lost her passport (been there!).
- Twenty-two-year-old hasn't sent off some vital forms in time.

Your child will always feel safe to come to you with difficulties, even when they've done something foolish! Hardwiring the habit of offering empathy in all situations keeps our bridge in tact. It allows

a child's PreFrontal Cortex to get lots of practice at solving, resolving, rationalising and reasoning. *They* will learn that your love and connection doesn't get taken away when they've made mistakes and that you will be there to walk with them no matter how big or small the problem.

They will realise that they don't need to 'act out' to be heard and understood. And *you* will learn what troubles your child and how they process their challenges. No matter how pressured the situation, we can afford a little moment of empathy. Our first response will set the trajectory for the conversation and for the relationship.

"It's a mighty act of human love to remind people that they can accomplish things for themselves." - Elizabeth Gilbert, author

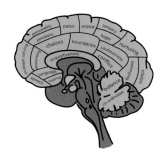

OXYTOCIN

Oxytocin is a feel-good hormone that is released from the pituitary gland when we experience the feeling of love or bonding. Sometimes it's called the cuddle-hormone. It can be stimulated by feeling nurtured, such as having a hug, a connected conversation, focussed time with someone, words of encouragement, a gift or being the recipient of a kind deed. It's also the hormone released during sex or breastfeeding. It's a strong hormone. In fact, it's the one that stimulates childbirth contractions!

When oxytocin is released, a person experiences an increase of affection, contentment, calm, love, generosity and trust. It also has the benefit of reducing fear and uneasiness, which can lower stress and blood pressure and even reduce cravings for sweets, alcohol and other addictions. Marketing companies have worked this out and provoke its release to sell products by offering us inclusion and connection. This causes a response of trust and generosity which can prompt us to purchase.

Children of all ages crave releases of oxytocin. If they don't get it at home, they will seek it elsewhere. A recent study has shown that oxytocin levels increase when tweeting, using Facebook and socially interacting in cyberspace. Oxytocin is now available online!

Our time, affection and attention as parents isn't just nice, it's what our children need. Their innate desire for oxytocin, even if they've never heard of it, is what motivates them to bond and build connection. Their primary source needs to be from their parents.

Examples

Here are some extra examples from clients and friends who have used empathy.

LEARNING TO LISTEN

Recently, I went for a walk with one of our children who was facing a difficult issue. It was so tempting to wave my Mummy wand and advise, console, offer him a treat, or reason that the problem was manageable. But this was my moment to validate his emotions and build security and trust. It was his moment to be understood, where he could grow his own solving muscles, rather than have me iron things out. I didn't want to miss this.

I listened to every detail (gold star) and empathised with his concerns. I had a little guess at his feelings, which helped him to name them, so I affirmed them. Then I listened again, rather than advising. About an hour later he told me he felt so much better. "What made the difference?" I asked, feeling a little chuffed. "I had something to eat," he said.

Dent in my pride! But, I doubt that food would have felt so good if he hadn't had his feelings understood, accepted and validated. He went on to say what he felt would help his situation.

OUR LITTLE SPACE

Remember Helen from earlier in this chapter? Her son had issues at school and she'd given him great advice. She recently sent me this:

"Some time ago you advised me to let my son talk about the problem and make time and give him space to say why he is feeling the way he is. This little 'space' of ours works to this day as he responds really well when we have our one-on-one chats and I understand why he sometimes gets angry or why he reacts in a certain way. He still struggles sometimes with the playground politics but feels much more at ease and knows that he can come home and be listened to."

FROM TEARS TO BRAVERY

A little boy had spent some time doing a painting when the water cup was knocked over and spilled all over the artwork. His mum's instinct had been to say, "Don't worry, you can do another one. It'll be okay." But she tried her listening skills and said, "Darling, that's so sad. You must be so disappointed, you'd spent so long painting that."

Through his snuffled tears he said, "It's okay, I could get some more paper and do another one."

PAYING ATTENTION

Not long after we had our second child, our two-year-old developed some uncharacteristic behaviour which was obviously attention-seeking in nature. As he couldn't voice his frustration eloquently, I sat down with him and took some guesses at how he was feeling. It became clear that he wanted a bit of time with me, away from the baby. At first I thought this might require a big effort, but it didn't take much to affect his behaviour. He was happy with the odd ten minutes playing Duplo together or sharing a bath with him when the baby was napping, but I think his behaviour changed because I acknowledged the issue.

IT'S NEVER JUST 'FINE'

I was sitting having a cuppa with a mum when her four-year-old fell over and had a very small knock on her knee and came running to her mum. Instead of saying "You'll be fine," the mum responded with great empathy and understanding. The little girl quickly recovered and returned to her game. I know it's only a tiny example, but her little girl will learn over and over again that she can trust her mum not to minimise her feelings.

IN A NUTSHELL
UNDERSTANDING FEELINGS

- Most issues, whether big or small, feel extreme to young people
- If we want our children to share, we need to listen without judgement
- The brain is not ready for advice until the emotional distress has been empathetically met
- It's tempting to clean up their muddle and move them on
- A child's trapped emotions can lead to self-soothing in order to numb the pain
- Empathising is accepting someone else's perspective, regardless of whether we agree with it
- Empathy validates our children's feelings and allows them to process their pain
- It is the key to emotional intelligence
- When children feel safe, they will share and explore their options
- When they've considered their options and made a plan, resist the urge to give them a better one. Gently ask questions about any potentially unwise choices
- Empathy takes courage. If we empathise, our children will share with us and even allow us to influence them
- Empathy keeps the bridge clear for both of you to cross

The Power of Humility

Have you ever met people who just can't be wrong? They're quite hard work, aren't they? One of the qualities I hope my children will have is the ability to own their issues, acknowledge their shortcomings and humbly apologise when they've upset someone.

In order for that to happen, we need to make our home a safe place to go wrong. When they make mistakes, as they will, it's so tempting to lecture and correct or make them feel ashamed. But if we want to grow children who own their mistakes, we need to accept apologies and show mercy. If we enable our children to see that they are lovable and acceptable, even when they've made mistakes, they will be able to own their issues and offer authentic apologies, both now and when they are adults. If we accept a genuine 'sorry' (not to be confused with sorreeeeeey), they will be able to own up and say sorry because they will learn that an apology is acceptable in your home.

It doesn't mean we're not allowed to have feelings. But there are ways to let them know we're struggling with the effects of their choice at the same time as appreciating their apology. If the remote control is broken because it was slung against the wall in a moment of frustration, we could react with, "I'm really upset that it's broken, but thank you for your apology." It doesn't mean they're excused from restoring the damage. It just means that there is peace in the relationship. One of ours found recently that riding over a white carpet in rollerblades leaves a bit of a mess! The apology has been genuinely accepted, but there will be some cleaning up to do.

Children who have their apologies accepted become more responsible adults. They don't live in order not to get caught and they are able to face their mistakes because they've learned from their parents that love is not withdrawn when they mess up.

I knew of a mother who pretended she didn't notice when her son made mistakes. In order to shield him from any consequences, she lied to her husband to cover for her son. As the son grew older the mistakes got bigger. In fact, they became

illegal! As kind and accepting as it may feel to that mother to overlook her child's misdemeanours, the message she is actually sending is that she can only love the pretend version of her son; the real one is too hard to face. That is not unconditional love. If sorry, forgiveness and mercy are part of family life, we will raise children and adults who are not afraid to own up to their mistakes and face their poor choices. They will see that our love is not conditional.

MODELLING THE HUMBLE APOLOGY

It won't always be our children that make mistakes. How we respond in times of error will make a strong impression on our children. Sorry is not an easy word. Do you ever feel tempted, when you say sorry, to follow it with a justification? I remember, quite some years ago, apologising to one of our children, who was about eight at the time. I was tired and intolerant, and something made me snap. I wanted him to know that I was sorry, but also for him to understand what he had done that triggered me. So, I began an unhumble apology that started like this:

"I'm sorry, but..." Being agile with words, he quickly cut in, "A sorry butt is a sore bottom." Cheeky! But true. There are times to let our children know we're a bit shredded, or that we're not coping as well as we might normally, but letting them know their part in our mistake is not an apology. In the words of Abraham Lincoln, "Never ruin a good apology with an excuse."

The way we accept their apologies will influence the way they will accept the poor actions of their siblings and others. It doesn't mean we expect them to be doormats and let people go wrong with impunity. It just means that there's room for relational restoration before the clean-up process begins.

We will all have experienced, at some stage in our lives, a humble apology. It's sad that they're not more common, but isn't it powerful when it's authentic and when it's not followed with an excuse? You never know – if you model genuine apologies, they might come back your way too.

"Those who think forgiveness is a sign of weakness, haven't tried it."
- Archbishop Desmond Tutu

CHAPTER FOUR – CHOICES

Room to Grow

An enormous apple tree from a neighbour's garden overhangs two little stunted apple trees in our garden. The trees have taken on bizarre shapes to get the light and space they need. They cannot grow up so they push out in odd directions but remain very short.

Whilst we can prune, stake and protect trees, ultimately, if we don't give them enough freedom, they will be unable to develop to their appropriate height and maturity.

Freedom

There are so many advantages to being young. Whether our kids are two or seventeen, they are free of the burden of a mortgage or rent, filling the fridge and up-keeping a home. But whilst they're not in charge of the big stuff, they can feel like they are not in charge of anything.

Having no choices is not only limiting, it can cause power struggles. To quote Cat Stevens, "From the moment I could talk, I was ordered to listen," can be the story of childhood: brush your teeth, put your coat on, get in the car, eat up, settle down, wait! Make your lunch, put your shoes away, clear your room, hurry up, be back by, get up by, don't be late, put your phone away, stop complaining, speak nicely, have you done your chores?

Every day is filled with words; words of suggestion, words of expectation, words of limitation. Even if they're said gently and kindly, they're still instructions. The frequency of them can cause our children to feel herded. What if we replaced some of our instructions with options? Then their overriding message would become one of freedom over their little or large responsibilities.

Does freedom mean we shouldn't have boundaries and expectations? Of course not: there's a whole chapter on it later. Freedom isn't about permissive parenting. There are times when children need a specific instruction. We shouldn't be afraid of using appropriate authority to steer and guide them. This chapter is about offering some wiggle-room within the boundaries so the children are more likely to focus on their options than their limitations. It only requires a small change in the way we speak to our children.

WITHOUT CHOICES	WITH CHOICES
To a small child: Pop your coat on, we're leaving soon.	We're leaving in a few minutes and it's raining. Would you like to take a coat or an umbrella?
To a tween: Please empty your lunch box.	Would you like to empty your lunchbox or put your coat away first?
To a teenager: Please can you take the bin out.	Would you like to take the bin out now or after dinner?

"It's in the context of choices that character is formed." - Bill Johnson, author and leader

Freedom empowers people. It implies trust, whereas commands are decisions made for them. That may not seem important over the small issue of putting on socks, popping rubbish in the bin or heading for bed, but there are many words in a day and many days in a childhood. The words we choose create the atmosphere our children live in. They can experience an atmosphere of freedom within safe boundaries or they can experience a list of instructions, which can feel constricting.

You might be wondering at this point if anything will get done if the children are given choices over everything. I accept it's far quicker to just roll out commands. But take heart, your children will get better and better at making choices as they learn what to take responsibility for. You may find you'll need to slow down a bit so they can catch up.

Response-ability

Responsibility is response-ability. Our children need to practise choosing responses. When we trust them to do this it sends the message, "I believe you can do this." The younger we start giving them options instead of orders, the greater the sense of freedom and responsibility they will grow up with. However, it's never too late to start.

It's our role as parents to show them how the home works and what's expected of them; it's theirs to decide whether to rise to the challenge.

We can offer them chances to respond well by turning our suggestions into questions.

The cost

I know from experience that as parents we all feel passionate about different things and there are some areas where it is harder to give our children realistic choices.

Will they have a messy room if I don't nag? Get a detention if I don't chase? Forget to feed the rabbit if I don't persist? Go out without a coat? Not eat enough breakfast? Miss the bus? Appear on your Instagram story with mismatching clothes? Yes, it's all possible when we step back and give them choices. But it's in this space that they develop responsibility. You won't know what your children are and aren't capable of until you give them room to fail.

Each area could be a chapter of its own as parents struggle to get their children to be ready on time, eat their food, speak respectfully, do their chores and come home when expected. If there are battles over these areas, the chapter on Consequences will be helpful (see Chapter Seven). This chapter is about a change in narrative, a loosening of the strictures, space to get it right all on their own and yes, space to go wrong. Giving them choices won't turn them into responsible children over night, but living with more freedom (within the boundaries) is a tried and tested way of setting them on a path to responsibility.

Parents who have moved across to freedom and away from commands haven't always found it easy at first. In many cases they've had to slow down in order to leave time for these choices. They've had to bite their tongues as their children have had the freedom to make good and poor choices. But those who've managed to relinquish control all report a change in atmosphere in their home and a rise in responsibility. I've also noted, as time's gone on, these children don't end up in teenage power struggles with their parents. Where there's an atmosphere of freedom, there's less to fight about.

I found there were areas where I had to learn to be less prescriptive. The amount of (well-thought-through) freedom children have will impact their character and their relationship with you.

The fewer areas you give them for rebellion, the fewer potential threats to their connection with you and others.

"When a person feels that he is truly accepted by another, as he is, then he is freed to move from there and begin to think about how he wants to change, how he wants to grow, how he can become different, how he might become more of what is he is capable of being."

- Thomas Gordon, pioneer in communication skills

The main battles

FOOD

One of the areas that is hard to ease up on is children's eating habits. I realise we're responsible for a balanced diet and good nutrition, but forcing children to eat is the beginning of a power struggle. It's possible to set some firm boundaries and then offer choices within them. For example, you choose the time for a meal, the amount of snacks in the day as well as the ratio of savoury to sweet. Then they can make their choices within those limits.

If the emphasis on mealtimes is time together to chat and catch up rather than just re-fueling, then the focus is taken off the food. If they don't eat much, they'll learn from the experience of being a bit hungry.

The way our children eat at home and the atmosphere around food will influence their relationship with food for the rest of their lives. Being forced to eat might satisfy you as a parent for that mealtime, but it won't have a positive effect on their future diet or your relationship with them. In fact, getting frustrated with them about food gives them a control area. What a fun game for them. If they're feeling the need to gain a little power, this might be an easy win for them.

HOMEWORK

This is one of those areas where we can get a little muddled. We want our children to get their homework in on time and done well, but is that to ensure they are performing well or because their efforts feel like a reflection of our parenting? Who can say? But one way or another there are some great cases out there of parent-homework – ask any teacher! Much of the work sent home isn't just to stretch and train their minds; it's to get them to work independently. Leaving them time to work alone develops independence and responsibility.

TIMEKEEPING

Here's an area that makes parents dance. If we tell our children when we're leaving and then fly around grabbing coats and shoes, shuffling them towards the door in a hail of frustration, it's just possible that we're not offering them choices here. (Refer to Consequences, Chapter Seven, if it's a persisting problem.)

TANTRUMS

(I'm not just talking about small children here!) Most children will try a good strop when they want their way, but whether or not they make a habit of it depends on how we respond. Cajoling them out of a tantrum teaches them that it's a good

"Sometimes it's the smallest decisions that can change your life forever." - Keri Russell, actress

way to get our full attention, so does arguing. Giving in speaks for itself. Another way is to offer empathy for a moment by saying, "I understand this is hard," or "I'm sorry you're struggling with this." Let them know that you're ready to listen when they're feeling calm and move away. That leaves them with a choice.

Giving a child options won't mean bamboozling them with choice, but it will entail small choices throughout the day in place of commands.

FOR LITTLE ONES

- Would you like to pour your cereal or shall I?
- Do you want your toast cut into squares or triangles?
- Shall we go to the park before or after the shop?
- Would you like to brush your teeth before or after the bath?
- Which pyjamas are you going to wear tonight?
- Shall we chat then have a story, or have the story then chat?

PRIMARY SCHOOL CHILDREN

- Would you like to wear your coat or carry it?
- I understand you're frustrated, but would you like to behave nicely or take your frustration to your room?
- Do you want to lay the table before dinner or clear afterwards?

When they're getting up and down during dinner:
- Would you like to stay at the table or eat on your own afterwards?
- Shall we have peas or broccoli with tea?
- Would you like to continue that discussion (argument) with your brother in the hall or the garden?

OLDER CHILDREN

As we move into the tweens and teens they become freedom fighters. The more options you can find the better.
- When's a good time for you to hang the laundry, now or in 15 minutes?
- This Saturday, would you rather mow the lawn or clean the car?
- Shall we spend some time together this evening or at the weekend?
- Would you like to catch a lift with me now or catch the bus in your own time?

There are so many areas of their lives that are tempting to manage: how they handle their money, their friendships, their sports commitments. Giving them choices develops them. Involving them in our planning gives them a sense of freedom too. Instead of handing out chores, how about having a list of chores and asking them which ones they'd like to do?

Ask them whether they'd like to help you plan the meals for the week ahead or make decisions about cereals, snacks or fruit.

On paper it can all feel like minutia, but every sentence goes into the bank of words they hear that day, that year. Children will develop differently depending on the daily narrative they hear. Offering options builds mutual respect. It enables them to feel a sense of collaboration. It develops their ability to take ownership for their lives and to exercise their brain's frontal lobe where they can consider their options. Above all, it reduces their need to exert control as they don't live with a sense of powerlessness.

DOES ANY OF THIS MATTER?

It matters enormously. I can't put too big an accent on it. Parents I see on a consultancy basis report great differences when they decide to replace instructions with choices. The atmosphere and culture in which we bring children up has major effects on who they become in a few short years.

"*Life is the sum of all your choices.*" - Albert Camus

Examples for offering choies

INSTRUCTIONS	SUGGESTIONS
Get dressed	What would you like to wear today?
Put your shoes on	It's sunny today, flip flops or shoes? or Would you like to put your shoes on here or on the stairs?
Get in the car	Would you like to take a toy or a book in the car with you?
Jump in the pushchair	Would you like to take a banana or an apple in the pushchair to eat on the way?
Finish your breakfast	I'm clearing breakfast away in 10 minutes.
Be quiet	I'm happy to read the book when you've finished talking.
Clear away your bag and shoes	I have some cakes at the table for when you've put your bag and shoes away.
Clear your room	You can clean your room any day this week before Saturday lunchtime.
Hurry up	We're going to leave at 4, what do you need to do to get ready?
Do your homework	Would you like to do your homework before or after tea?
Don't wear socks in the garden	Would you like to wear shoes in the garden or have bare feet?
Bring your laundry down	Feel free to bring your laundry down as often as you like. (ie, it doesn't get done unless they do.)
Take that ball in the garden	Would you like to play with the ball outside or with a different toy inside?
Be back by	Let's agree a time for you to be home.
Don't be late	If you're home by that time, you can stay out that late next time.
Put your phone away	Feel free to check your texts after dinner.
Speak nicely	I'm ready to talk about that when your tone is gentle.
Have you done your chores?	When would you like to do your chores?

IN A NUTSHELL
CHOICES

- Giving no choices can cause power struggles
- Character is formed through choices
- Giving children freedom doesn't mean a lack of boundaries, it's just offering some wiggle room
- Culture can be changed with a little change of narrative
- Every sentence we speak goes in to the bank of words they hear that day
- Freedom is empowering
- Giving choices means taking longer – everybody has to slow down a bit
- Children will mature if they're given room to succeed and room to fail
- Offering options builds respect
- Choice builds responsibility

The Power of Compromise

I remember when our eldest was about two and he went off for the afternoon with my husband for some man-time together. When they got back, he proudly announced he'd had his first fast food meal. That had not been part of my dietary plan for our children.

It didn't occur to me, as I glided up the aisle; I never thought, as we watched that precious first baby-scan; I had no idea, as we brought our darling bundle home, that we, as parents who seemed to share so many values and dreams, could possibly have some big differences of opinion.

If there's one thing that parenting highlights, it's that whilst we share many values, we also have very different ones. These can show up in a myriad of ways. Perhaps your differences are over organic food or what the children should wear, where they go to school, or whether they should go to bed on time and in which bed!

Whilst our personal values are important, if we don't compromise with our partner, we're not sharing the parenting role. If there are two of you, it's healthy to bring both of your influences to the family. If we give each other space to bring our different styles of parenting to the family we are raising, we end up with a unique blend of influences and an unspoken respect for our partner.

"You've got to list your priorities before you live your priorities."

- Ken Costa, philanthropist

CHAPTER FIVE – DIFFERENT WAYS TO LOVE

The Right Nutrition

Our home came with a greenhouse and I decided, in a moment of enthusiasm, to grow just about everything. It wasn't long before our greenhouse overflowed with little pots of small green shoots and the time soon came for them to be transplanted. I laid them all out in the garden to decide what should go where and then went to put the kettle on for a well-earned cup of tea.

That was my big mistake. When I came out again our toddler proudly brought me a large handful of labels. Not a single plant remained named and I had no clue which was which. Without any differentiation at all it was impossible to ensure each plant got the right amount of shade, sun and the specific type of soil and nutrients it needed in order to flourish.

When our children are small, we instinctively hold them, cuddle them, give them our time and constantly encourage them. In fact, if you're reading this and have very small children you may find it hard to imagine that may ever dwindle. But as they start to get a little older and more independent, it's easy to forget how much of us they still need, especially as they don't appear to. Then, when the teen years kick in, they can fool us into thinking that their greatest needs are being met outside the home. However, whilst the attention from their friends is more alluring at face value, what they really need is *our* attention. They just don't know it in quite the same way as they do when they're little.

A person's brain is not fully developed until they are in their early to mid-twenties (see page 54). Children and teenagers are not mature. They won't always opt for what they need. If they did, the sale of vegetables would go up! Our children will turn to their interests and their friends, which is healthy, but their greatest needs still come from us and there are many ways to continue to make them feel loved.

I found Gary Chapman's book, *The Five Love Languages*, pivotal for understanding the different ways our children like to receive love and I highly recommend it. I'm going to use the same themes to explore love languages and how that can help us connect with our children. From time to time I host groups of mums in my home and we go through these concepts. Sometimes there are tears of relief as they have revelations about themselves, their partner or their children and the different ways they express and receive love. Understanding love languages is a powerful tool for understanding ourselves and others.

The basic concept is that there are five common ways to offer and receive love. Gary Chapman lists them like this: Quality Time, Touch, Acts of Service, Gifts and Words of Affirmation. These are like the nutrients we put into our plants.

Re-fuelling

Love, just like nutrients, gets used up. Chapman talks about our children (in fact, all of us) having a tank inside us which parents can fill with love, but that also gets drained each day. Have you ever felt you're just giving out and giving out and not being refreshed? Everyone's drawing off you but you're running on empty? Our children can feel the same way. Their problems may look smaller to us, but they feel just as draining and significant to them.

Time

Here are some experiences that drain their tanks:

- Impatient words from a sibling or parent (no judgement here)
- Unkindness from a friend
- Sternness from a teacher
- A fall
- A fail
- A panic
- Being left out
- Being hurt
- Being overlooked (when we've run out of steam or we're too busy or forget to meet their needs)

Each little challenge takes a little from the tank. So how do we fill the tank back up again? Well, interestingly, different children have different needs. A parent, with all their love, can replenish their child's tank. Without that restoration, the child can become agitated or anxious because they've run out of fuel to draw from. All five types of love will replenish, but after reading this you may begin to notice that one or possibly two of the 'languages' seem to have a special power for different children (or our partner, friends and family; this is a versatile tool). Let's look at all five ways of expressing love.

We know our kids need our time, but it isn't always easy; there's a house to run, possibly a job, not to mention the extra curriculars and other pursuits. It's for this very reason that we need to be intentional about spending time with our children because days, weeks and months can easily whizz by as one busy demand is followed by another.

Paying attention and being interested whilst making eye contact, rather than multi-tasking, nurtures them. They'll often be around us when we're busy, but stopping what we're doing and engaging with them feeds their soul. Having dinner together without screens, phones or other distractions builds connection.

There are many ways to spend quality time: playing boardgames, bike rides, rollerblading, walks, creating traditions, planning days out, sharing dreams or concerns and scrapbooking with them are just a few ways to refill their tanks. As they get older, this time together evolves; I find that food is usually involved with our teenage boys. And they're never really too old for tucking in at bedtime, although sometimes mine have to tuck me in these days.

"Children spell love T-I-M-E." - Rob Parsons, speaker, author

*All children love our time, but if **quality time** is your child's top love language, that time will have extra power to release oxytocin (see page 61) which will deeply nurture them. They will also begin to show signs of depletion if they haven't had that **quality time** from you.*

One of our children loves rollerblading and one day, I fell for the idea of going to town with him on our blades. That mile felt like about ten and we still laugh about what happened when we hit the downhill. The story gets bigger and bigger – I never 'faceplanted' that shop window! The child who loves time is often the one hanging around you whilst you're cooking or otherwise occupied.

Touch

I'm sure one of the reasons we come into the world tiny is so that we can be held so much. The importance of touch is not lost on a parent. Our toddlers and young children love hugs and they initiate physical play partly to get that contact. However, it's easy to underestimate a child's ongoing need for touch as they get older. They don't seek it as much and can even look as if they're not craving it. Don't be fooled. We just need to be a little creative about how to offer it as they might not scoop neatly onto our laps like they used to.

Banking a good few moments of physical contact during the day has an impact on their emotional growth: goodbye and hello hugs, morning and bedtime hugs, kisses on the cheek, a hand on the back or a kiss on the head, wrestling, high fives - they all add up. Mine all love a back rub, one loves silly handshakes, two of them will still put their head on my lap in the hope of having their hair stroked. But one of my boys will give me a bear hug at least a couple of times a day. For him, touch has power.

However, there are times when older children may avoid touch. Don't take it personally when it appears to be rejected, it could just be timing or mood. Older children will often soften at bedtime and allow parents to snuggle in, read with them or chat about the day when they know that bedtime has struck and all other options are off the table.

*If **touch** is your child's top love language then touch says, "I love you," whether that's a cuddle or rough and tumble. If they lack that **touch**, you'll start to see the cracks. The lack of contentment and calm might show itself in their not-so-admirable characteristics. That's the clue that their oxytocin level is running low and they're in dire need of your **touch**. If they don't get it from the safe arms of a parent, they may seek it elsewhere.*

The child who loves *touch* is often affectionate with others and particularly younger siblings.

Acts of service

As a parent, you are probably serving from dawn till dusk (and dusk till dawn some nights). But *acts of service* are a little extension of that. They're an offering that says, 'I thought you'd appreciate this...' Whether that's bringing a child a hot chocolate or snack as they're doing their homework, helping them to find an item they've lost, tucking a water bottle into their bed or doing something for them that they're usually expected to do themselves.

In our home that could be making their packed lunch, hoovering their room, making their bed, unpacking their layer of the dishwasher or doing their dog walk for them. The words 'Let me do that for you' can have power.

If one of your children's love language is *acts of service* they are touched when someone thinks to take something off their list or do a random act of kindness. This replenishes their tank, destresses them and makes them feel loved. They can interpret lack of effort from others as lack of care and love. Doing little things (or big things) for that person sends the message, 'You matter to me'.

All children love a room cleared by a parent, but for one of our children, it doesn't just clear their head (and their room), it seems to fill their heart. It does take a bucket of grace on my behalf, but I know that when they're having a tough week, or going through exams, it changes their world.

The child who appreciates *acts of service* is often found doing thoughtful things for others and will go out of their way to take a task off someone to lighten their load.

"The first and most important choice a leader makes is the choice to serve."

- Robert Greenleaf, writer and philosopher

Gifts

All expressions of love are gifts in their own way but I'm talking about physical gifts here. The sentiment of a gift can feel more significant than the gift itself because it says, "I was thinking about you". But the reverse is true too: a poorly thought through gift (I'm sure we've all had one of those) is worse than no gift. Gifts don't have to be expensive, but thoughtfulness has great value.

If *gifts* is your child's love language it doesn't mean they're materialistic, they just respond to the thought that is behind a gift and a present can fill their tank and replenish them when they're feeling drained. If gifts isn't your love language it can be hard to rise to the challenge of filling this child's tank because it can seem trivial. Keep a note of the things they love and accumulate a list of things you can give.

I have a child for whom gifts are powerful: if I pick a few fresh flowers and leave them in a jar by his bed, or buy a small bar of chocolate for him, he feels loved. For another child, gifts don't fill the tank: I cleared her room once to find unopened gifts! She's not ungrateful, but far more affirmed by time.

The child for whom *gifts* has power often loves giving gifts themselves. However, it does not always mean it's their top love language.

Words

Who doesn't love a kind word? Little comments about how well they did, or somebody noticing that they've thought beyond themselves, feels particularly precious to a child whose love language is *words*. Appreciating their efforts, kindness or a way that they've managed themselves has power if it's well supported appreciation. "You're fab," is nice, but it doesn't really cut the mustard for a child who loves *words*. Specific positive feedback from you, a coach or teacher or friend will really stoke them up. Reminding them of the good characteristics we see in them can re-affirm their identity (especially when they haven't been their best version of themselves that day). It nourishes. They will be impacted by written words too – notes in lunch boxes, under pillows, letters, a note after a disagreement, a thoughtful text message, a card left in their room if you've gone away.

Those for whom *words* of affirmation are their top love language will feel a flood of contentment when they experience someone's authentic appreciation of them. They're not hunting for compliments, they just feel more loved by *words* than action. Your encouragement will pour into their heart. Interestingly, they can be easily crushed by words too, so after any honest parental feedback it helps if it starts and ends with some affirmation.

One of our children particularly loves *words* and during exams I'd put little Post-It notes in their room saying 'Keep going'; 'You're doing so well'; 'We're so proud of you'; 'Love you'. When I cleared their room after they left home recently, I found that all the notes had been kept. They matter.

I've noticed that the child for whom *words* are significant often enjoys *words,* writing, making up words and learning new words.

Children are nurtured by all expressions of love and under the age of about five they need all of them so much that it's quite hard to discern which one they favour. But as they grow it usually emerges that one has a turbo boost. There are online questionnaires you can fill in to work out which you, your child or your partner is most nourished by. It's worth saying that love can never be formulaic, children are intuitive enough to know whether we're ticking a box or offering something from the heart.

Taking time to make that genuine offering in the love language they respond to best can make them feel especially loved, which leads to contentedness, optimism and all the things that make them extra delightful.

"Kindness is a language the deaf can hear and the blind can see."
- Mark Twain, writer

IN A NUTSHELL
DIFFERENT WAYS TO LOVE

- We are the greatest nourishers of our children's hearts – no matter how important their friends may be
- Love can be put into five main expressions: Quality Time, Touch, Acts of Service, Gifts, Words of Affirmation
- We need all types of love but, quite often, one or two ways have the power to change our day
- As our children are drained during the day from their challenges, we can restore them with our love
- Love can never be formulaic, but the right nutrient can restore our children's peace and sense of contentment
- Children are the best version of themselves when they feel loved (we all are)

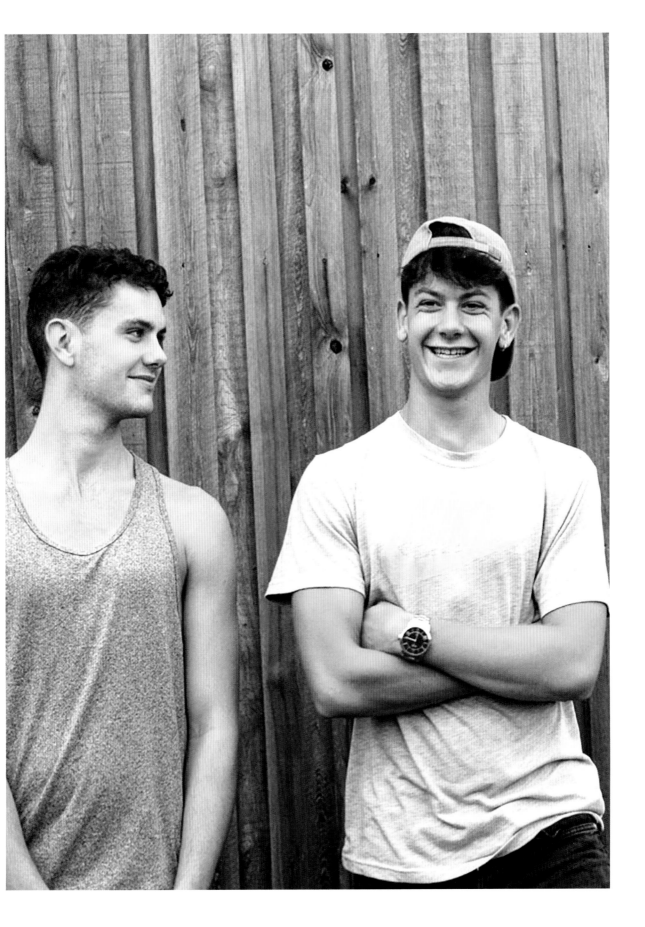

The Power of Rest

There was once a very ambitious woman who was trekking in Africa. She hired some locals to carry her goods and on the first day she managed to get her helpers to move at a good Western pace.

On the second day, none of the Africans would move, they just sat. No matter how much she tried to motivate them, they refused. "We are letting our souls catch up," they said.

Do you ever feel your life whirls by? We live in an incredibly busy world. Demands are constant. Today's child is educated earlier, has to process much more information from the world around, hears more voices and has a much busier diary than children from previous generations. There's a danger that we find our significance in being busy and wear it like a badge of honour or that we get overloaded and let the 'urgent' get in the way of the 'important'. Yet, we need rest, we need to let our minds, bodies and souls restore. It actually improves our overall output. It's wise.

We can counterbalance the hectic world our child grows up in by ensuring there's a balance between work and rest. We can practice downtime. But it does take practice, because it's countercultural and can get easily hijacked by the to-do list.

Rest can sound boring. What thoughts does it conjure up for you? Sleep? Screens? Boredom? Lolling around? Reading?

Rest can be a time when we stop being busy and put our feet up, if we dare. That enables our children to see us stop and it also leaves time for them to learn to resolve their own boredom. A headmistress recently told me that she and her staff

have had to come up with something called 'The Wow Factor'. They have found in recent years, that children joining Reception Class have been so overstimulated as preschoolers, that keeping their attention requires something magnificent to happen every fifteen minutes. Having gaps and spaces that they learn to fill-in for themselves is part of their development.

RESTORE THE SOUL

But rest can also be doing an activity that restores the soul. It can be making time to do things you love (aside from work, even if you do love it). Intentional time to enjoy the family; a time where you avoid the shops, phones, social media and chores.

For some, that will be going for walks; playing with the kids (like they do in books and films and that we mean to but don't quite have time for); watching a film; chatting (not about the tough stuff); going for walks, even in sunny, crispy winter; a bike ride; a day trip; having meals that last longer than the eating. Rest can be about being together, undistracted and giving our children our focused attention. It releases oxytocin (see page 61).

Rest helps us to restore mind, body and spirit and enables us to be kinder, more patient, more fun and more creative. This affects how we feel about ourselves and impacts everyone around us, particularly our children.

It's not easy to rest, but if life is balanced in such a way that it isn't possible, then I would dare to say, it's out of balance. Our children will pick up far more from our behavior than from our instruction. If we want them to leave home knowing that rest is important, then we need to be intentional, even a little excited, about rest.

"If your output is greater than your input, your upkeep will be your downfall."
- Richard Hubbard, songwriter

Strong Love

BOUNDARIES

CONSEQUENCES

SURVIVING CONFLICT

SIBLING CLASHES

SOCIAL MEDIA

Pruning

A number of years ago, friends of ours, Rob and Marianne, moved from London to a house in Somerset that had a garden which opened to the public during the spring and summer. We were all a bit surprised as they barely kept a pot plant alive, but they were soon awarded medals and the garden was featured in well-known magazines. In a recent conversation Marianne shared that their brutal use of pruning had been one of the key factors that enabled their garden to flourish. She learned first-hand that nutrients were easily wasted if plants were allowed to get gangly and leggy. So, she diligently cropped them back – to virtually nothing!

Love has many guises. There are times when it is soft and comforting and there are times when it is strong and it cheers a person on to be their best. This is where pruning comes in. Sometimes our children can be like those little seeds in the opening chapter, craning to grow faster than is good for them, passing by the boundaries, leaping over the well-thought-through, age-appropriate limits. It is in these times that our role is to bring them back to a place from where they go on to flourish, even if they don't appreciate the delay!

CHAPTER SIX – BOUNDARIES

Fences

In a study, some preschool children were taken to play in a local playground where there was no fence. The children remained huddled around their teacher, fearful of losing sight of her. On another day, the same children were taken to a similar playground where there was a boundary fence. In this scenario, the children spread out and played, feeling free to explore within the given boundaries.

The conclusion was that the children felt safer to explore with a set limitation, knowing that they were in a safe environment within the boundary of the fence. Without a boundary, the children were more reluctant to leave the caregiver and felt less inclined to explore.

Boundaries are defined limits and expectations. Everyone has them – in their work, family, at the school gates and in all their relationships. Have you ever felt disappointed or wondered why someone behaved in a certain way, like interrupting or pulling out of a commitment? It's likely they've crossed a boundary line that matters to you.

At times I'm grateful for boundaries. I'm aware that the limits and expectations of traffic lights increase efficiency and decrease accidents. I felt my son was protected when the football player who broke his nose was banned from playing. I'm pleased I can say 'no' when I don't agree with something. I have an expectation that people pick up mess after their dogs!

A world without boundaries could be a bit of a mess (literally at times!). Yet, at other times, I resent them. Why do we have to drive at a prescribed limit or pay for parking in our own town? Our task as parents is to have expectations for our children and limits as to what we will allow them to do. Our children's task is to butt these boundaries to see if they are secure.

Children who have grown up with secure, age-appropriate boundaries find it easier to form relationships when they are young and throughout adulthood. We probably all hope that our children will make good, lasting friendships and be a pleasure to work with and live with.

It's much easier to teach a child healthy boundaries than let them learn as adults. I'm sure we've all come across controlling characters or those who dominate or create opposition, even when it doesn't seem necessary. During their childhood they didn't learn to respect the limits of others.

We've also come across people who are too eager to please or even exhaust themselves running around for others, wanting to be needed. They didn't learn enough about healthy expectations during their childhood. Teaching our children about limits and expectations is a gift to them that will last throughout their whole lives. If they are shown healthy boundaries they will learn to protect themselves physically, mentally and emotionally. But how they are taught is important too. In this chapter I give some examples of parenting styles and the impacts they will have.

There are three or four main parenting styles that are often referred to when talking about boundaries. The four that I use are influenced by some of that research, but also by experiences shared with me by many parents. These insights have also been used for the examples given in each category.

Controlling – using pressure or force (sometimes called authoritarian or disciplinarian)
Nonchalant – lack of boundaries (sometimes called uninvolved or permissive)
Over-attentive – always assisted or rescued (sometimes called hovering or indulgent)
Soft/Strong – freedom with age-appropriate guidance and boundaries (sometimes called authoritative)

Controlling

When my son and I used to cycle to school in the morning, we would take a short cut through the station, where cycling is not permitted. I'm a bit lazy, so we would pedal on through regardless. However, if we noticed the station police on patrol, we would get off our bikes and walk through the gates like model citizens. I didn't want the hassle, or the fine! That's control and it works.

CONTROL ERODES RELATIONSHIP

When we obey in order to avoid punishment, it's called control. Control works like a dream - as long as authority is present. Have you ever slowed down on the motorway when you've spotted a police car? It probably wasn't because you suddenly appreciated the wisdom and sense of 70mph! Control through force and punishment is an effective method for law enforcement. It also works in schools and throughout many institutions. I've discovered, to my detriment, that it works in families too. Control works, but there's a cost – control doesn't build connection and trust: it commands, which over time will erode relationship with our children.

When we over-manage our children, our focus is on them learning to obey, not learning to reason, problem solve and self-manage. They need space to evaluate right and wrong and to weigh up the risk against the benefits.

Zac and Nadia are polite, compliant children. They stay well within the boundary lines, because either their parents are watching or they know there will be strong repercussions if they don't! They check their parents' expressions before they make any decisions, even small ones, and they find it hard to raise objections to anything. They're not developing the ability to make good choices because they aren't trusted to use trial and error or to experience the natural effects of choices - either good or poor ones. Their ability to develop intuition and initiative is being hindered.

As time goes on, Zac and Nadia may make lots of poor choices because they've not had enough practice at making decisions, they've always waited for command or approval.

As adults they may have low self esteem because they haven't built confidence in their ability to make good choices. This will affect their relationships. They may try to control others at home and at work because they've learned that overpowering people gets results. Excessive authority is a short-term strategy. It may produce compliant children for a while. But well-behaved children aren't necessarily happy and emotionally healthy. Controlling parenting hinders the child's sense of being an individual. They're more of an adult-in-waiting. They can develop fear and shame through conditional acceptance.

"Yes officer, I did see the 'speed limit' sign, I just didn't see you."

Nonchalant

A number of years ago, our family flew to a little island in a light aeroplane. The seating arrangements obscured the pilot from our sight, but Tom (age three) and I had a terrific view of the ocean. For some daft reason, I told Tom that the lever by the side of his chair was for steering the plane. I explained that it would make the plane go left, right, up or down. "Drive safely," I cautioned.

At first he loved it and held a steady course. But, as we began our descent, the angle of the plane made it look as though we would land in the water. He pulled madly on the lever, but down we seemed to plunge. He panicked, cried and begged me to take the control.

PASSIVITY ERODES GROWTH

Kids would love to be in control. They may even convince you that they should be. The reality is, they're not ready. They don't have the wisdom or the maturity to manage their lives without our guidance and healthy boundaries. I guess that's why the job of raising them is given to older people who can teach them to take increasing responsibility, up until they're ready to be launched into the world.

There are a number of reasons why it could be appealing to allow a child excessive freedom. Perhaps the parent has greater priorities and is overlooking the child's need for guidance. It's also possible that lack of knowledge or confidence in parenting has lead them to feel that their children will just learn to manage themselves.

The needs and wants of children are not the same. Consideration and respect are not instinctive – they're honed. We have the ability to gift our children with these values through guiding them with age-appropriate boundaries.

Children of all ages will press against the boundary lines to see that they are firmly in place. Psychologists tell us that children will interpret healthy parental limitations as love. They will press and press until they find it.

Joseph and Taylor had really 'relaxed' parents. Their mum would often say, "There are no rules in our house!" They weren't expected to help in the home. There was no pressure to return items they'd borrowed and they were thrilled that the usual boring restraints that other children had to put up with didn't apply to them.

On the surface it looked great. However, behind closed doors rows often erupted. Joseph and Taylor saw their parents as weak. They were disrespectful and inconsiderate and made poor choices with impunity. As time goes on, Joseph and Taylor may

Over attentive

learn not to respect any authority, not even healthy authority. It will be hard for them to master age appropriate self-management because they've not had clear expectations.

As adults they may feel that their internal happiness and self esteem is derived from having their own wishes met. They may strive to meet their external needs in pursuit of happiness. They may resort to manipulation or lying to get their own way, which will affect their relationships and their choices.

Nonchalant or 'laid-back' parenting is another short-term strategy. It may be easier to give in to children's expectations than to love them through the disappointment of a healthy limitation or expectation, but it won't grow them.

Children will grow to look like adults, but without the experience of healthy limitations and expectations, they're still a three-year-old inside without the tools to make wise decisions for themselves and for the sake of those around them.

There was once a little boy who saw a butterfly struggling to get out of its cocoon. He kindly tore the cocoon open a little and eased the creature's passage. When the butterfly emerged, it lacked the strength to fly and soon died. The vital struggle of emerging develops strength and forces fluid through the wings so the butterfly can stretch and take flight. The little boy, in all his kindhearted sympathy, had in fact impeded the butterfly's advancement, so it lacked the necessary maturity to survive.

HOVERING ERODES RESPONSIBILITY

Some parents want to be friends with their child or over support them. They find it hard to allow their children to be accountable for their own choices. They ensure their needs are always met and their mistakes are always covered which may involve running forgotten items to school; doing their homework; whizzing them here and there or rescuing them from the latest emergency due to the child's lack of planning. The little opportunities for learning experiences are seen as imposters.

"Gentleness is strength under control." - Elizabeth George, author

Jordan and Sam's parents want their children to have a happy childhood filled with a world of opportunities. The kids are the King and Queen of the family. With their parents' close attention to their every need, they are developing a CV of all-round success. Their parents want to protect them from disappointment, so they defend them from teachers who don't understand their individual needs. They cover up their failures and ensure misdemeanors are re-marketed as misunderstandings.

Jordan and Sam will be fine until life poses challenges from which parents can't rescue them. When problems at university, health challenges, relationship and employer issues are beyond the reach of parental micro-managing, they won't have had the years of practice and development that childhood was supposed to offer them.

We all love our children. But part of loving them is allowing them to grow, even when that's a little uncomfortable. We can see by the effects of the above parenting styles that the way in which we approach boundaries with our children will have a huge impact on their characters, their values, their achievements, on the friends and partner they choose and on their career.

Children are not born with the ability to self-regulate. Limits are a gift which will protect children physically, mentally and emotionally. If we protect them with fair, consistent, age-appropriate boundaries, which leave them space to make choices and even fail, they will rise to self-regulation. They will also learn to set appropriate limits in their own relationships which will protect them and others. Expectations are a gift. We have a great opportunity in the home to teach them to be responsible about telling the truth, being timely, helping in the home, doing homework, helping others and contributing generously in all their different spheres.

Soft/Strong parenting

PARENTS ARE VISIONARIES

Expectations and limits will vary from home to home. We expect our children to take their shoes off before going upstairs but that might not be an issue for you. You might not let your children drink that last bit of milk from the cereal bowl, but as it doesn't bother us, it's not a boundary we uphold (though I don't blame you if you don't want to come to our house for breakfast!).

Responsibilities will be things like:
- Speaking to each other respectfully
- Helping in the home
- Going to bed on time
- Doing homework
- Paying debts
- Managing social media responsibly

Interestingly, some of the limits will be much the same, but perhaps just expressed differently:
- Don't push, shove, shout or mock
- Don't use abusive language or label people
- Don't take things that aren't yours
- Don't lie or cheat or manipulate
- Don't be late

Parents are visionaries. The boundaries they choose will be based on their desired outcome for their children and home, depending on their particular values.

CLEAR COMMUNICATION

Explaining why a particular responsibility or limit feels valuable in your family is more helpful than just a straight 'yes' or 'no'. So many children are bemused about why the lines are there. If boundaries are not well communicated they can become invisible expectations.

I was involved in a survey a few years ago where we asked teenagers what they thought their parents' values were. There were many misunderstandings. In the absence of parental explanations, children will make assumptions. One child had thought that her parents' boundaries were largely in place for her to attain high academic marks, which wasn't, in fact, the parents' highest goal at all.

I remember one of ours saying, "The reason you set us chores is so that there's less for you to do." Well, that's true in part, but it isn't my motivating factor. In fact, don't you often find it's a whole lot easier just to do it yourself? Setting chores trains them to have good domestic skills and be thoughtful in other people's homes as well as their own. Sounds like I needed to explain that value.

REVIEWING THE BOUNDARIES

It's helpful, from time to time, to re-evaluate where the boundary lines are placed so they remain age- and maturity-appropriate.

With our eyes on the long-term, we're looking to raise children who will make good decisions later. For that reason, they've got to practise making some, even if it feels uncomfortable to let the boundaries out. Over the years, some of our boundary lines got a bit stuck in the mud. It was through occasional discussions with the children that we reconsidered some of our limits and made the leap of trusting them with that next stage.

A forest school teacher was observing how children responded to boundaries and noted that when they have completely exhausted the area they're restricted to, children will begin to breach their boundaries.

Revisiting where the boundaries are placed gives our children the message that the lines are well thought through. Sometimes it confirms to us that they're in the right place. When one of ours was 13, he asked us to look at a game rated 15 which he felt was too high and showed us evidence that many parent-reviewers felt the same. We took a closer look and on this occasion, we didn't move the boundary, but he felt we'd given it the attention he'd asked for.

I look back now and am relieved that we kept some boundaries firmly in place and moved some when prompted. And of course, there are some we regret. The eldest child usually has to watch the youngest one having wider boundaries than they'd had because it's not just the children that are growing, we're growing too. Whatever we do, it's healthy for children to know that they are free to discuss their feelings and that boundaries do move with age and responsibility. If children can learn to politely challenge their parents, they'll gain the confidence learn to appropriately challenge and contribute to positive changes in their different life contexts.

We should be secure enough for our children to challenge our boundaries (nicely). It's their way of asking 'why?' It doesn't mean we have to change the boundary line. We just need to listen and let them know we understand their frustration and, where relevant, let them know we'll think about it. This way, they learn to respect authority, not fear it. They also learn that hearing people's perspectives doesn't mean you must give in.

It's also our responsibility to model boundaries, not just dictate them. Children see, children do. We'll never be perfect, but if they can see us being responsible about the way we speak to our partner and friends, being timely, returning borrowed items, being careful with our belongings and if we're keeping our rooms tidy (bit of a stretch for me sometimes!), managing our finances and restraining ourselves on social media, they're far more likely to respect the boundaries.

HOW WE COMMUNICATE

The tone and words we use impacts our relationships with our children. If we're barking orders or repeating ourselves, then they learn that they don't have to respect the boundaries until we're jumping about and raising our voices. I know we've all had moments we regret, but if this is a habit, it's a powerless way to parent. It's controlling and it destroys bridges.

Setting boundaries for children is really just teaching them to tend their side of the bridge (see page 13). and not to violate the other side, then helping them to carry that principle across to all their bridges (relationships).

We can do this by communicating our boundaries clearly, being empathetic with our children's frustrations and modelling responsibility.

With all that in place, they will still make poor choices from time to time. The chapter on Consequences (see Chapter Seven) offers ways to let them learn from experience rather than forcing changes. If we keep dashing across the bridge constantly correcting, averting mishaps and not giving them the space to go right and make mistakes, then it's hard for them to build the muscles they'll need to manage themselves. The next chapter will show how we can be both strong and gentle at the same time as we inspire them to respect our boundaries.

"Happiness isn't a goal, it's a by-product of a life well lived." - Eleanor Roosevelt

IN A NUTSHELL
BOUNDARIES

- Boundaries are defined limits and expectations
- Everybody has boundaries – even laid-back people!
- Boundaries can both protect and frustrate, but a world without them would be confusing
- If we want our children to feel empowered to protect themselves, then we need to show them boundaries
- It's easier to learn healthy boundaries as a child than to learn them as adults
- Control erodes relationships
- A lack of parental boundaries isn't 'chilled', it's weak
- Passivity erodes growth
- Micro-managing erodes responsibility
- Boundaries and limits are gifts
- Boundaries are based on your values
- Parents are visionaries; they have a desired outcome for the character of their children

The Power of Grief

Grieving can be uncomfortable. Grief isn't just about death, it covers so much more. It's sadness about any loss, whether that's a loved one or a pet, the loss of a precious soft toy, a job or even a place.

SHARE YOUR TEARS

Sometimes we think we're protecting our children when we hide our sadness from them. A parent once said to me that they didn't want their children to see them cry. If we don't share a little and make grief acceptable, they won't learn how to process loss. If they see us shed a few tears, they will use their instincts to comfort us. We don't have to sob uncontrollably and make them carry the burden of our sadness, but we can allow them to see some vulnerability.

Many people who have faced deep losses have been hurt by how their friends respond or even avoid them. Those friends probably weren't shown as children how to respond to loss. They may well be afraid of it. If loss is pushed under the carpet, our children won't know how to face it when they encounter it, and may end up hurting people.

DON'T HIDE TRUTH

It's tempting to hide news from our children that might make them sad or anxious. But if we do, we're missing an opportunity to walk with them and help them to grow. Journeying grief is healthy. It could be that we are afraid of holding their pain because we can't take the source of it away. Our children are more likely to emotionally survive grief if they're allowed to experience it and learn to trust us to comfort them through it.

CHILDREN CAN COPE WITH LOSS

When adults face loss, it can feel overwhelming, like we're wading through a river of pain. Children handle grief more like puddle jumping. One minute it matters, the next minute they've moved on to something completely different. "It's so sad about Dave's cancer, please pass the ketchup."

LET THEM ENQUIRE

It's important for them to know that questions are permissible, even if we are not always able to answer them; sometimes there just aren't any good answers.

Over a lifetime there will be wonderful moments, but there will also be loss, sadness, illness and pain. Burying pain doesn't make it go away. Share loss, share feelings and let your children be comfortable with vulnerability. It's part of growing together.

"You're braver than you believe, and stronger than you seem, and smarter than you think." - Christopher Robin

CHAPTER SEVEN – CONSEQUENCES AND RESPONSIBILITY

Deep Roots

As Morag and I sat with our cup of tea overlooking her beautiful garden, I asked whether watering the garden was a full-time job. She answered, "I never water the established garden. I water the new plants, but then I peter out their dependence on the hose or they would not bed down deep roots in search of water for themselves: they would stay at surface level where they would expect to have the work done for them."

As tempting as it is to help our children through everything, they can't develop responsibility unless they are left to make choices and experience the consequences.

Occasionally, it's just possible that our children might mess up or leap across our boundaries. This is a good time for a well-thought-through logical consequence. Consequences is the most misunderstood of concepts and it's the one I'm most often asked to speak on. When a parent visits me to share a struggle from their family life I'll sometimes ask if they use consequences. They usually say that they do. I'll ask for an example and they normally give me a consequence that doesn't relate to the boundary line that is being crossed: taking their screen time away is a common favourite. With respect, if the consequence isn't linked to the issue, it's a punishment.

We're equipping our children for life and life has logical consequences. For example, if I forget to put out the bins, nobody comes and switches off my Wi-Fi. The consequence is that I have a week of overflow and potential to attract rats or mice. Nobody tells me I can't go out on Saturday night.

Similarly, it's not logical to make a child's bedtime earlier because they hit their sibling or to take a teenager's phone away because they insulted you. A logical consequence is something that flows naturally from the choice.

For example, for little ones, it might be that you give them 15 minutes to get ready for bed and have a story, but if they use it all up getting ready, then the logical consequence is that there isn't time for a story. Sound harsh?

Bear with me – pruning takes a bit of courage!

Logical consequences allow our children to decide for themselves whether they like the outcome of their own choices. It's hard to stand back and allow them to make mistakes and experience the difficulties that come with poor decisions, but it does enable them to evaluate the outcome. If they make a better decision the next time, it's because they've decided to, not because we're telling them to. It takes patience because learning is a journey.

The instant gratification of getting cross with them or forcing an outcome isn't actually teaching them; it's control.

"Anger short-cuts learning ." - Jim Fay, presenter, author

Letting go of the reins

Control works. Punishments, ultimatums, threats and shouting will get results. Many parents will admit that the morning drill alone can include raised voices or threats of computer time or other privileges being taken away, and perhaps comments that are regretted later. After all, we're only human.

A child will respond to control by obeying just as long as you're either watching or likely to find out later. However, whilst children may obey to avoid parental repercussions, they are not developing character (they're also becoming immune to your outbursts). This style of parenting will not exercise their brain's PreFrontal lobes, where options and possible outcomes are considered - they're just obeying in fear of reprisal. This can cause resentment and distance in the relationship like rubble and rust building up on the bridge.

As controlled children grow, they learn to control. This can produce stubbornness which can become full-on defiance by the age of twelve. Some might say that *all* teenagers have a rebellious phase, but I'd say that is not the case; it's a self-fulfilling prophecy that's bandied about. Yes, they grow in independence, but I know many families, including our own, where the children haven't been through a rebellion. We can hope for something different. We can set some logical consequences for different choices and allow the consequences to do the teaching. That leaves us free to be gentle and empathetic through their disappointments and failures.

Moving from the certain world of punishments and control to the more spacious world of consequences requires us to stand back and allow them to make choices. That's not always easy. Let's face it, we quite like holding the reins. If we allow children to make their own choices they might make bad ones! Will they eat too slowly, or not enough? Might they be rude or forget to clear up their mess or tidy their room? Will they get down from the table before dinner? What if they forget to wear a coat or go to school without a PE kit or lunch? Will our teenagers stay out late and make their own rules? What kind of a home will we run if choices prevail?

In the short-term, standing back and allowing them to walk in the effect of their choices may well mean that they make a poor choice. But the chances are they'll only make it once or twice. You won't be nagging them on the same point for six years. For example, I was getting a bit frustrated with our children forgetting their door key and constantly having to drop what I was doing to go and let them in. As petty as it felt, I changed tack and went to the door to let them know I'd go around and open the side gate. It was a bit of a performance, and more inconvenient for me in the short-term, but they soon got weary of it and now, hey presto, they remember their keys.

For each area you would like them to mature in, you can have a logical consequence that will teach them far more effectively for the long term than nagging, cajoling or swooping in to cover their mistakes. Let the effect of their choices do the teaching. Learning by experience is so much better for our relationships than nagging.

This might be a little messy at first, but it doesn't mean that life will become chaotic. You don't need to tackle everything at once. There are some areas where your children will be showing natural responsibility and other areas where you'd like to see some progress.

For example, one of our children was always under-prepared, so he often left things behind in the hope that we'd swiftly courier them to him. Yet he was responsible about time-keeping. So we allowed him to forget his things, stopped whizzing them across to him and let him walk in the consequences, but on the rare occasion he was late we didn't feel the need to set a consequence because it wasn't a habit.

Another of our children was the exact reverse. They had everything ready, labelled, boxed and bagged, but were always running late. On the rare occasion they forgot something, we'd help if we could because this wasn't a characteristic that needed pruning, it was an oversight. However, I wouldn't jump in the car to drive them somewhere if they were running late, because they needed to walk (possibly literally) in the logical consequence of their habit of lateness.

One of my clients had a teenager who was constantly late and causing her mum to be waiting in the car. She decided to calmly time her daughter's lateness. She then asked for that child to repay the time debt when she returned from school by doing some chores. Time re-paid for time that was borrowed.

The point of consequences is not to find another method of control, it is to allow them to learn where they need to mature. For those areas, it's helpful to work out a reasonable, respectful and related effect which flows naturally from their choice.

"Comfort is the enemy of progress." - Phineas Barnum, showman

Cause and effect

In some cases, the effects will choose themselves. For example, if a child leaves their PE kit at home and you don't run it in to them, there might be a natural repercussion at school.

However, in other cases, the consequence will fall to the parents. For example, if a child is misbehaving at dinner, it's not helpful to threaten the loss of their bedtime story – it's not a natural repercussion. A logical consequence would be to tell them that they're welcome to stay at the table if they can behave nicely. Otherwise, they can leave the table and eat on their own after you've all finished. You may need to follow through by removing their plate (and even the chair).

My kids had a habit of leaving their shoes in the hallway. Five kids with sports shoes, school shoes and boots etc soon had the hall looking like a charity sale. Whenever you hear yourself repeating a request, that's a good time to stand back and consider a consequence.

This was my consequence: I offered them the choice of clearing their shoes away or leaving me to clear them. Then I began taking them to the shed at the end of the garden and lining them up nicely in there.

They'd come looking for their shoes. I would explain that they'd made the choice of leaving me to clear them away, which I'd done, very neatly in the shed.

Soon there were little panics just as they were running out of the door: "Where are my rugby boots?" "Who's seen my sliders?" "Has someone borrowed my trainers?"

It's hard not to enjoy this moment because it makes for quite good theatre. However, smirking smugly in the hall as they dash around in a panic isn't helpful.

The effect inside the boundary line: you find your shoes in your cupboard.

The effect outside the boundary line: you'll need to walk a bit further to get your shoes (possibly trudging through a wet garden).

You can be a people lover without being a people pleaser

Keeping calm

When our children make their choice, it's important to keep calm and respectful and let the consequence do the teaching. That's empowerment. Don't try and persuade them to rethink, just follow through with the consequence. Empowered, effective parenting isn't loud.

If I were to shout angrily up the stairs, "If you don't put your shoes away right now I'm going to go and shove them in the shed", I would be back to nagging. That's disempowered and no fun at all. We tend to nag, shout or complain when we feel powerless. Sarcasm isn't helpful at this point either, nor is a smart retort:

- *"Well, I wonder why I put them there!"*
- *"Maybe you'll learn for next time!"*

As tempting as those responses would be, they are not respectful and they're not necessary if we are empowered. In fact, this is our opportunity to be empathetic with their situation. We're in a far more objective place to do that when we're standing back and allowing them to take up their responsibilities whilst we're carrying out ours.

If we spare them our wrath, we get a chance to show unconditional love by remaining kind, regardless of the choices they make. It's harder and requires more patience but it keeps our bridge in tact. The consequence will be enough in itself. After all, we are on their side. We'd love them to learn to put their shoes away so they're easy to find. However, it's up to them. You're showing them how your home works best for everyone and that they're welcome to fall in...or out. That's responsibility; they do their side of the bridge, leaving you free to do yours.

BE PREPARED FOR THE BACKLASH
Children will resist logical consequences. It is so much easier for your child if you're in a spin. Not because they like to be shouted at, or watch you grip your own head and dance around the kitchen in sheer frustration, but because when you're *out* of control, they're *in* control.

I'm not sure what your child's response would be to hearing that their shoes are down the garden, but they're unlikely to say, "What a cracking idea!"

"And you ask 'what if I fall?' Oh, but my darling, what if you fly?" - Erin Hanson, poet

It's more likely to be:

- "You did what?"
- "Wouldn't it have been easier to 'pop' them in my room?"
- "Why do you have to be so difficult?"

This is their attempt to bait you into their pit of frustration. Spare yourself. Take a breath and pour in empathy and love because you are not trying to win a game or shame them into submission. You're simply showing them how your home works and that they're welcome to make their choices within it.

CHOOSE A ONE-LINER

It's worth having some one-liners at the ready so you don't get caught on their bait and reeled into a debate:

- "I understand that's frustrating."
- "I'm sorry this is hard for you."
- "Let's chat about this when you feel calmer."

"It's not what you do for your children, but what you have taught them to do for themselves, that will make them successful human beings." - Ann Landers, columnist

Logical consequence

Thinking up a logical consequence isn't always easy. You might be brilliant at thinking of them on the spot. We initially found it was a bit of a head scratcher. They had to be:

- Safe
- Enforceable
- A natural outcome, linked to the behaviour
- A choice, not a manipulation

Consequences can soon morph into ultimatums or punishments if we're not careful. One parent said to me recently, "I try to link everything to the phone and use the phone as a consequence." Not helpful! Remember that in setting a logical consequence we're maintaining a value, not looking for revenge or control. Consequences come out of a desire to grow them, punishments come out of a desire to even the score or force an outcome. If it's not logical, it's not a consequence!

When we began to use consequences, we shared the idea with a couple of friends who decided to do the same. We used to phone each other for consequence inspiration over different scenarios.

If you can't think of a consequence on the spot, give yourself time to form a plan. Let a child know that you're disappointed with their behaviour (not disappointed with them!) and that you're going to have a think about what to do about it.

For example, if they haven't tidied their room by the required time, you could do it for them and then they could return the time spent by doing a chore for you. Choose one that's less appealing than clearing their room: leaf sweeping or bathroom cleaning.

You won't need a million consequences. Most flash points in family life are repetitions – lateness, untidiness, rudeness and laziness. Not all of them will be poor habits, some will just be oversights. You'll know by frequency which ones require a consequence to be set. I had to trip on a number of shoes before I realised we needed to get thinking about an enforceable, logical consequence.

Moving away from the reliable world of punishments and force, to the vulnerable world

---

"Sooner or later everyone sits down to a banquet of consequences."

- Robert Louis Stevenson, author

of allowing our children to make choices, is a change in trajectory and will take time to learn. There will be days when we just misfire or haven't got the patience. We're all fallible; nobody's got the whole thing taped. It's not just the kids that are growing - we're growing too! But as you gain experience in standing back, letting them make choices and having some logical consequences ready, it will become a natural way of thinking.

Consequences don't guarantee immediate results. Strong, gentle parenting is a process. When our children are given space to make choices, they will make some good ones, but they will certainly make some poor ones. At which point, celebrate (quietly to yourself). Because every lesson they can learn in your home, is a lesson learned whilst the stakes are relatively small and there are loving arms to scoop them up. As they build muscle in these areas, you are saving them from far greater repercussions later because they would have taken that poor habit into adulthood with them.

A friend of ours confessed, after he'd been unfaithful to his wife, that his parents covered up all his mistakes through childhood. He had never learned how to cope with failure and disappointment, they just felt shameful. So when his marriage had issues, he didn't know how to face the problem so he avoided it.

RESIST THE SHORT CUT!

Setting consequences is more time-consuming. It's a long-term strategy, but it's often harder than just solving the short-term issue.

- It feels kinder to run an item to school than to allow them to get a detention.
- It's easier to remember to grab their coat or a snack than leave them to remember.
- If they've broken something they've borrowed, buying a replacement avoids awkwardness.
- If they miss the bus, they may well miss a sports lesson that we've actually paid for, so it's easier to drive them.

It's far quicker to swoop and cover their mistakes than to allow them space to experience the effect. It's much easier to put the shoes in their room and clear up their toys than be trotting down to the shed. But, when we swoop in and cover for our kids, we are usually paying the debt for them. This is confusing for them whilst they are developing the concept of responsibility.

It's so easy for a child or teenager to assume that everything that goes wrong is someone else's fault. When their sports kit isn't through the wash, they're running late, they've lost something, it's tempting for them to shout for us as though we're a genie in a magic lamp. It's equally easy for them to pass the blame when they've bumped into someone, for example: "You shouldn't have been standing there."

How often have you heard people pass the blame? Making a clear divide on the bridge between their responsibilities and yours means that they will become aware, through repetition, whose responsibility is whose. If we are taking responsibility for their side of the bridge, it won't be long before we're exasperated, and saying things like:

- *"I've told you a million times."*
- *"Can't you remember your own things?"*
- *"I can't believe I'm doing this for you again!"*
- *"When are you going to learn to be responsible?"* (Possibly never.)

Frankly, the child begins to fade out the parent's voice. As one mother said to me, "My voice is just white noise in our house."

The benefits

Moving across to consequences was revolutionary for us, but it wasn't always easy. We had to watch the children building muscle in weak areas and hold our tongues! But interestingly, from that moment onwards there was no need to shout or persuade. There was a plan and we felt empowered and able to empower our children to rise to their own responsibilities.

It's hard to let a child miss breakfast, leave their project at home or run out of clean tops because they didn't bring their laundry down. But when children are given space to make choices, they feel the freedom - they also learn that failure is just part of the journey, it's not shameful. If our children are allowed to make poor choices and still have our respect, love and support then they will grow in confidence.

When children grow in responsibility, they make good choices when we're not even looking. They are strengthened and equipped from the inside rather than just experiencing external pressure. They develop strategies for life as they use their rationale and reason to consider possible outcomes, rather than just being told what to do.

Setting logical consequences is part of strong love. Just like pruning, it allows short-term discomfort for long-term gain. Pruning strengthens the plant and enables healthy growth and, ultimately, yields more fruit. However, setting consequences can be hard. It can feel like a step backwards at first, as there is no immediate gratification. In fact, it will cost you popularity at times. But parenting isn't about gaining our children's approval, it's about raising good characters who will know freedom and responsibility.

"Responsibility finds a way. Irresponsibility makes excuses."
- Gene Bedley, national educator of the year, pioneer

Examples

Here are some examples from clients and friends who have shared their consequences with me.

THE MORNING DRILL

My six-year-old refused to put on his school uniform: he wanted to wear home clothes to school. I gave him the choice of getting changed before the car journey or getting to school and my enlisting the help of his teacher. He chose the latter. The result? He got dressed quietly and calmly in the Headteacher's office (with me there) without any resistance. He decided he didn't want that to happen again. From then on we never had any conflict about what to wear for school, and now we laugh about it!

BEDTIME

My ten-year-old has always fought against heading upstairs at the end of the day. Rather than getting angry, I told him that when it was time for bed I was available for 15 minutes, after which I would be going downstairs to get on with other evening jobs. I then went and sat on his bed and waited quietly. He went from running round the house and hiding and refusing to climb the stairs, to getting himself ready for bed in five minutes and joining me for his story.

TIMELINESS

One dad tried to tell his sixteen-year-old many times about coming out of school on time but he never did, so the father and the other siblings would wait and wait for him in the car. One day he drove off without his son. It was a calculated consequence and he was old enough to borrow
some money and get the bus home. The dad didn't lecture or huff. In fact he empathised with his son's wasted time on the bus. The son chose to be on time for his lift from then onwards.

MUSIC PRACTICE

Our son wanted to learn the saxophone, but didn't want to practise. We tried to coax him but it became a regular battle. Then I decided to step back and give him a choice. His lessons were £14.00 so I let him know that he was welcome to practise every day, or not, but for each practise he missed he would need to pay two pounds towards the lesson. He was cross and said that he was only learning it for my sake, at which point I said that wasn't necessary and offered to phone the teacher and cancel the lessons. He refused my offer and decided to start practising the saxophone!

STICKY FINGERS

Our four-year-old refused to use cutlery, he preferred to use his fingers. I didn't want sticky fingers all over him, me and the chairs so I gave him a choice. I told him that he was welcome to choose whether he'd like to use the cutlery or his fingers. If he chose his cutlery I would be able to sit next to him whilst he ate, which he liked. If, however, he chose to use his fingers, I would chose to sit at the end of the table where I could be sure of keeping clean. He was most put out when I sat at the other end of the table and opted for the cutlery. That was the end of sticky fingers at meal times.

CLEARING UP TOYS

One mother shared that she found the mess of toys upsetting at the end of each day. Cajouling them and repeating herself became exhausting, so she said, "You can keep the toys that you pick up." The rest she boxed and popped in the loft for a month. The toys were soon missed and she empathised with the kids. The next time she said, "You get to keep the toys you put away," her voice had a whole new weight to it. After a month she offered them a system of being able to retrieve the toys by doing some chores. She's not completely unreasonable, but she is enjoying them taking responsibility at the end of the day for their mess. She's even noticed them encouraging visiting friends to put toys away after they've finished playing with them.

FOOD BATTLES

Our eldest son was two and a half when he started becoming fussy about his food. Mealtimes were beginning to be a battle-ground so we asked for advice from a friend who was a paediatric doctor. He suggested that we give him a couple of food options at each mealtime, then leave the food there for about 10 minutes and let him know that he has a choice of whether to eat it or not. He assured me that after a few meals, as long as I didn't offer him snacks between meals, he would begin to eat again. If I hadn't tried this I would have become fearful about whether my son was eating enough and mealtimes would have become 'him versus me'. I first tried it one evening and he chose not to eat, so I cleared the meal away after 15 minutes. Throughout the next day he ate one or two spoonfulls at mealtimes, but very little. I held my nerve and didn't try to talk him into eating. On the third day, he came into our room first thing in the morning and asked for food. I put his usual breakfast out, which he would normally have refused. He wolfed it down and went on to eat three meals that day and from that day on. Looking back it was a power struggle and if we hadn't offered him a logical consequence we would have been bribing and coaxing him for years.

LEARNING TO REMEMBER

Another mum remembers when her ten-year-old son phoned her from the school office because he'd left his swimming kit at home. Her answer was, "Oh for goodness sake, darling, why did you do that (rhetorical I presume!)? I'm busy this morning, I can't bring it in."

"Then I'll have to sit with the Year Fives whilst everyone goes swimming," he complained.

She got very cross with him on the phone (rust setting into her side of the bridge, planting a few weeds; hazardous to cross) then begrudgingly agreed to take in the kit. She decided to try using consequences then next time. Sure enough there was a next time. Because he learned nothing from the last time, except, 'If I mess up, Mum explodes, then brings my stuff.'

Son: "Mum, I've left my swim kit at home."
Mum: "Oh sweetheart, I am so sorry."
Son: "Mum, you need to bring it in!"
Mum: "Oh darling, I can't, I'm busy today."
Son: "But Mum, they will make me sit with the Year Fives whilst everyone is off swimming."
Mum: "I'm sorry. That will feel awkward for you."
The school is only around the corner, but she had a vision for a responsible child. He never left his

swimming kit at home again. In fact, she recently noted that right through the rest of his school years, he very rarely, if ever, left anything behind.

LATENESS

Here's a funny story from our own family life, by permission of our 23-year-old. When he was sixteen he had the annoying habit of coming home late on a regular basis. When we told him that it was concerning, held up dinner plans and felt disrespectful, he told us to "chill". One night we were waiting up for him as he was supposed to be home by 10 o'clock. We phoned the mum of the friend he was visiting to see if he was still here. He was. My husband said, "Send him our love." He dashed home and made it up to our room by 10:30 pm.

"Sorry I'm late," he panted, quite out of breath.
"No worries," we answered.
He came back a few minutes later and asked, "Are we all good?"
"All good, sleep well," we answered.

*The next day we knew that he needed to be at football by 1:00 p.m. That was one thing he was **never** late for, because if you were late, you didn't get picked for the game (yes, the football coach was well ahead of us with consequences!). Before football we would all be at church and we were usually heading for the car by 12:15 pm sharp. But not on this occasion.*

I got chatting with a friend. My husband caught up with a few people. Our son, fully dressed for football, bags in hand, hovered, desperately trying to find a gap in the conversation to protest. Eventually he blurted, "Dad, we're late!"
My husband put an arm around him and said, "Darling, we've decided you're right. We need to chill a bit about time keeping."

His jaw dropped.
The penny dropped.
The bags dropped.

After 25 minutes my husband brought the car around and our son started hurling his younger siblings into it. I came out casually and realised that in order to stretch our lateness the full half hour, I had a few minutes to kill I said, "Oh, I need the loo." "MUMMM!" he wailed.

We didn't want to inconvenience the football coach, so we had texted him ahead of time.
Our poor son threw himself out of the car and ran towards the coach on the field, ready with his apologies, only to hear the coach say, "Yes, your parents said you'd be a bit late this morning!"

Whilst we laugh at this story in hindsight, the truth is it took quite a lot of nerve to carry out. We knew how important it was to him to be in the game and how stressful the situation would be for him. But we realised that in our frustration about his general habit of lateness, we had reverted to nagging and lecturing, which was eroding our relationship with him. We decided that the stress of one occasion was probably a fair swap for the years of nagging that potentially lay ahead.

PRUNING REQUIRES COURAGE

One lady recently shared that she'd heard a talk of mine on consequences some years back. At the time, she'd felt consequences seemed like 'tough love' and they jarred with her parenting style of meeting all her children's needs. She now says she wishes she'd left more spaces for her children to make choices, fail and build the muscle of responsibility. Her children are in their 20s now and she says she's watching them build muscle she wishes she'd let them develop when they were younger as the stakes that seemed so high back then, were actually small by comparison.

Those little challenges may become big challenges – exams, significant relationships and job interviews will come along. If they have not managed to 'try' independently, they'll be too anxious to rise to the challenge for fear of failing.

IDENTITY

If we can stand the discomfort of watching them fail, if we affirm their efforts and encourage them to try again, our children will believe that they are acceptable and lovable when they fail and when they succeed. They will learn that success and failure do not define them.

One of our children had a massive meltdown one day because of something they couldn't do. They'd left it too late and become overwhelmed. They cried, we comforted, they wailed, we gave them space. Eventually, with no other options, they began to work their way through it. The sense of achievement was palpable. They were in that happy little 'I did it' zone all evening. We could so easily have robbed them of that.

Handing them the responsibility is about making them realise the problem is theirs. We can load in the sympathy and love when they're walking through a consequence and send the message that we're not disappointed with them, we're disappointed for them.

That way, the relationship stays in tact no matter what choices they make. Children will even begin to use logical consequences with their friends which is so much healthier than people-pleasing or manipulation. One of ours had a friend who was consistently late and so one day she went ahead without her. It was a bold move and not popular in the short-term, but her friend wasn't late the following week.

"Start when they're cute, so they will stay that way!" - Jim Fay, author

IN A NUTSHELL
CONSEQUENCES AND RESPONSIBILITY

- Consequences are not the same as punishments
- Using logical consequences eliminates the need to shout, boss or control. It requires letting go of the reins
- Consequences are only necessary where character needs strengthening
- Consequences shouldn't be twisted into another method of control
- Using consequences requires courage
- Let the consequence do the teaching
- There's no need for sarcasm or lectures
- Soon your voice will have less volume, more weight
- The process can be hard as we watch our children build muscle in weak areas
- We may have to get used to being a little less popular, but it is a price worth paying for building our children's confidence
- Short-term discomfort for their long-term gain

The Power of Perseverance

Without even knowing it, we can be sending our children the message that their results are the most important thing to us. And in some respects, they matter greatly: we want them to meet their potential in sport, art, academia and other areas. But which is more important – their long-term character or short-term results?

When we encourage our children, we can affirm them for their results. However, there is more merit to admiring their perseverance, encouraging their ability to overcome failure, and affirming them for the time they've put into something. This will influence their attitude to learning and their ability to endure challenges:

- *"I can see that you've really overcome this struggle."*
- *"This was a hard test and I know that you put lots of study time in."*
- *"You've practiced so hard, I really admire your perseverance."*

There's nothing wrong with celebrating success, but if their end results trump their character contribution, they will silently pick up the message that the results matter the most. That may affect their self-esteem when they don't win or achieve the result they were hoping for.

It's not just me that has a preference for encouraging perseverance; it's scientifically proven to grow children's minds. The research of Dr. Carol Dweck at Stanford University has found that skill and intelligence can be developed and enhanced by effort. Dweck has found people who embrace challenges and bypass their perceived capacity will actually create new neurons in their brains: their brains expand! Of course, nature/nurture research will show that people do have natural ability potential. All the trying in the world might not see your child get an Olympic gold, but their potential will increase if it's not limited.

I was sharing this with a client recently and it inspired her to tackle her six-year-old's spelling difficulties in a whole new way. She no longer affirmed him for the results or showed her disappointment at the lack of good results. She simply encouraged his effort. Over quite a short period of time his whole attitude changed. His results did too, but that was not her highest goal.

Failure is not shameful. Walt Disney, Oprah Winfrey, Thomas Edison, Steven Spielberg, Colonel Sanders (KFC) and Winston Churchill are a few examples of people who chalked up epic failures before persevering all the way to success.

It's a shift in narrative for parents to celebrate struggle more than results. But it positively impacts the child's security and sense of worth. Little challenges will soon become big challenges – exams, significant relationships and job interviews will come along. If they have not managed to value their effort, they may become too anxious to rise to the challenge for fear of failing.

Children who learn to value perseverance learn not to fear failure and become strivers. They also learn that their parents' love and acceptance is not conditional.

"Success is not final, failure is not fatal: it is the courage to continue that counts."

- Winston Churchill

CHAPTER EIGHT – SURVIVING CONFLICT

Manure

Isn't it odd to think that horse poo could be nutritious? Talk about one man's trash, another man's treasure! Sometimes, if the wind is blowing in the direction of our house, it seems that all the farms of Gloucestershire have wafted in.

Manure is smelly, but it is rich with nutrients. Placing it around plants is not a pleasant job, but it helps them to flourish.

Conflict is the clash that can happen when people disagree. Some people enjoy it as a casual sport, but most people find it uncomfortable. I wonder if that's because it's usually handled so badly. Conflict can conjure thoughts of irresolvable differences, war zones, accusations, shaming and belittling.

Nobody likes criticism or hearing their children clashing with each other. If we could take conflict out of family life, we'd all find it easier. Yet, it's only through conflict and differences that our children will learn conflict resolution.

Family members won't all agree with each other 100 per cent of the time, so we have three choices when there are clashes in the family:

- We can overpower others.
- We can hide or suppress our unmet needs.
- We can resolve conflict healthily.

At home we have the opportunity to show our children how to resolve conflict and how to differ graciously so we can send them into adulthood with peace-making strategies. Peace doesn't mean agreeing on everything, it means gently understanding another person's perspective – even if you don't agree with it. Showing our children how to face and resolve conflict will enable them to become adept at listening, accepting, expressing themselves and peace-making, without being forced to agree.

Well-resolved conflict starts with two parties expressing their perspectives to each other. In the middle they share where they differ and why. And a happy ending would be compromise or understanding - even an apology on a good day, where relevant.

However, that middle bit can be messy because it's a place of uncertainty as different perspectives are heard, which can be unsettling. I so often find it's this middle ground that people can't bear. It can feel like a fearful, dark place where people get hurt and relationships get destroyed, so they choose to avoid or overpower the mess of uncertainty. But uncertainty doesn't have to be dark and fearful.

We can't always influence the way people outside our family respond to confrontation, but we can influence our own families to hear and understand each other. It's a bit like using manure: the process

"Conflict is growth trying to happen" - Helen LaKelly Hunt, therapist

can be unpleasant, but it enriches our children and their reaction to our input can produce good fruit. The best relationships are those where uncomfortable differences have been overcome. Other relationships where issues need to be skirted around or buried will have disconnections or 'don't-go-there' areas, which prevent genuine connection and deeper relationships.

There are two common types of conflict in the home between parent and child. One is when they are frustrated with our choices. Another is when we're frustrated with their choices. Let's look at the first one first.

1. When they are frustrated with our choices

No matter how well thought through and fair our boundaries are, we can be quite sure our children are going to be frustrated with their limitations sometimes. I'm sure every home is full of good examples. Let's say a child has told you they don't want to go to Uncle David's party on Saturday. Here are some common responses from parents.

Which one might you hear yourself saying?

- "It's important to go to family parties."
- "He's been a lovely uncle to you."
- "Uncle David is looking forward to seeing you."
- "I loved family parties at your age."
- "If you don't go to other people's parties, you can't expect people to come to yours."
- "It wouldn't be the same without you."
- "Don't be difficult."
- "I'll buy you a nice snack on the way home."
- "What's wrong with going to Uncle David's?"
- "You'll enjoy it when we get there."
- "We do lots of things for you, I want you to do this for us."
- "We've already accepted, so we're going."

Many of these are fair points and variations of them are also reasonable answers for most of our children's complaints. The problem is these answers are not resolving conflict. Each one shuts the conversation down. Whether by logical argument, distraction, humouring, rhetorical questions, analysing or simply name calling, none of them really engage with the child's concerns at a connected level and leave the child thinking:

- "You don't feel my issue is important."
- "You don't want to hear my problems."
- "You think I'm being difficult."

The reason I so often find parents close the conversation is because they can't see any point to the discussion if they're not going to give in to the child's request. Yet, there is so much point to the discussion.

Being heard and understood, even if it doesn't get you what you want, is much more relational than being shut down. Listening to a child's disappointment prevents disconnection. It is possible to engage with their frustration at the same time as maintaining the boundary line. Being prepared to hear their disappointments about bedtimes, chores, pocket money or mobile phones shows them that it's possible to have a calm conversation with someone who has a different perspective.

So how do we do that, when everything in us just wants them to do as they're told? It can be helpful, when they are aggrieved about anything, to have a default response so we don't fall into the trap of arguing or shutting them down when they express a complaint. One way to do this is to reflect. I call it *'Hunt the Feeling'*.
Here are a few examples:

- *"It sounds like you're frustrated that we have to go to Uncle David's party."*
- *"I can see that you feel overwhelmed by the task of clearing your room."*
- *"I can understand that you're annoyed to be missing bowling with your friends on Saturday!"*

If this is said with empathy, it won't sound as mechanical as it might appear on paper. Your child will either agree with you or correct you, for example, "I'm not frustrated, I'm cross." Or "I'm not overwhelmed, I'm just irritated." Being heard and understood makes a person feel accepted. If we accept a person's words, we accept *them*. One of our greatest human needs is to be accepted. Being unacceptable until we've changed, grown up or become compliant is a very insecure way to live.

Accepting a child's perspective is very different from accepting their request. Parents worry that if they listen to their child's perspective they'll get dragged into their pit of frustration or coerced into giving in. Be assured that we can accept our child's feelings, even when we don't agree with their view. We just need to come to the conversation genuinely wanting to hear how they are feeling and even offer empathy:

- *"I understand this is difficult for you."*
- *"Clearing up can be irritating and draining."*
- *"I can really understand how disappointing this is for you."*

By opening up the conversation, you take the issue from between you, where it sits like a black cloud, and put it in front of you both, so you and your child can both look at it together from the same angle. If you can understand the challenges it poses for them, then they might be ready to see how it looks to you. If they know that you're not going to be judgemental then they will be more likely to share with you, without too much drama or defensiveness.

Sometimes these conversations need to be postponed for a little. If they've aired their frustration just as you're about to get into the car or you're juggling ten other pressing needs, there's always a case for saying how important this sounds and making a time to chat about it at a later point.

There are also times when they (or you) need to calm down before having the conversation.

I realise at this point you've still got the messy room, Uncle David's party, the bowling issue or any one of a hundred other concerns that could come up in a day. As you chat with them, even if you don't feel it's right to change things this time, you can hear their frustrations and empathise with their difficulty. You may find that their perspectives influence future decisions. As in Chapter Three, once they've been heard and understood, they may come up with solutions or compromises. Either way, they will register:

- "You have a right to express how you feel."
- "I really want to hear your point of view."
- "Your ideas are worth listening to."
- "I want to understand you better."

- "I'm interested in you."
- "I might learn something here."

It is possible to understand your child's frustration or disappointment at the same time as apologising for not being able to change things this time. Conflict often becomes worse when we jump over this part and move straight to statements or solutions, which frustrate them, such as the initial examples that close off the conversation.

When their brain is overloaded with frustration, it operates from the Amygdala. This is the brain's fight or flight centre (see page 54) which produces reactions (rather than considered responses) such as stomping, raging or generally acting out the frustration they are not permitted to express.

The brain's PreFrontal lobe, where reason and rationale take place, gets hijacked. When our children are heard and understood, their issues have a better chance of bypassing the Amygdala so they will be more likely to exercise their PreFrontal lobe.

By listening to your children, even if their outcome remains the same, you're setting a culture in your home where it's acceptable to express feelings. If your home permits healthy cconflict, your children will be able to express their needs or wants in a calm manner.

2. When we're frustrated with their choices

They will learn that they are permitted to share that thay are disappointed with our choices and that we can cope with their perspectives. They will learn that they don't need to stomp and shout to be heard and understood because there is space for their perspective, even if it hasn't had the desired outcome. They will also learn that being calm is a better way to get your full attention. As you pause to understand your child, they will grow to trust that they can share their feelings with you.

They may need to take a little time to process their disappointment if they haven't got their way, but they'll also learn that sometimes you will alter course. However, they'll see you're far less likely to just because they're having a tantrum.

Trying to mobilise children to do the things you want them to do can be hard work. When they opt to run late, leave their things around, speak rudely to us, misbehave, play in the garden with socks on (again), or want to get another piercing in their nose, it's tempting to react out of frustration:

- *"You're not listening."*
- *"You're making us all late!"*
- *"I've told you not to wear socks in the garden."*
- *"You're all so noisy, be quiet."*
- *"I'm not letting you go out again if you can't get home on time."*
- *"Don't be rude."*
- *"You'll look ridiculous if you do that!"*

When children are accused, they will inherently defend themselves (actually, we all will). Accusations include the word 'You'. A more peaceful way to get the message across is to use the word 'I'.

Earlier in this chapter, we looked at when the children were frustrated with us and heard about the technique of *'Hunt the Feeling'*.

When we are frustrated, we can use the technique *'Express the Feeling'*, which sounds like this:

- "I don't feel I've been understood."
- "I get anxious when we run late."
- "I find it frustrating when socks are worn in the garden."
- "I feel aggravated when the noise is loud."
- "I worry about you when you're not home at the agreed time."
- "I get upset when I'm spoken to rudely."
- "I feel unsettled about you getting another piercing."

I realise that it won't make them magically start listening politely or be timely, quiet, polite and calm, but then neither will an accusation. This isn't a trick for getting them to behave beautifully; it's a way of being clear and replacing conflict with a path to resolution. Accusations produce defensiveness, which closes people down. Owning the feeling by using the word 'I' diffuses tension and opens up a way forward.

When children realise you're expressing your feeling about their behaviour, rather than your feeling about them, they'll be more ready to hear what you have to say. The next step is to express your needs:

- "I don't feel I've been understood, I'd like to talk about this."
- "I get anxious when we run late, I need to get to work on time/I'd like you to get you to school on time."
- "I find it frustrating when socks are worn in the garden, I'd like the socks to last longer."
- "I feel aggravated when the noise is loud, would you play in the garden/shut the door/ choose a quieter game?"
- "I worry about you when you're not home at the agreed time and would like to know that you are safe."
- "I get upset when I'm spoken to rudely, I'm happy to talk about this when I'm spoken to respectfully."
- "I feel unsettled about you getting another piercing, let's talk it through."

It's hard to believe that simply expressing ourselves differently can diffuse conflict, but it can. Expressing our frustrations and asking for our children's help in resolving our problem is very different from pointing the finger and blaming.

"Freedom is to live in a way that respects and enhances the freedom of others."

- Nelson Mandela

The effect is that children are less resistant because they don't feel attacked.

They're more likely to listen and take responsibility for their behaviour. That won't always be the case; if they're spoiling for a fight, they'll try and bait you. But using 'I' instead of 'you' defuses and is less confrontational.

If children have a repetitive issue that you feel does need tackling, consequences are a helpful, non-forceful way forward and more effective than nagging. But if something needs saying, the most helpful way to let them know you're frustrated is to take the YOU out of your sentence. This shows them how to express themselves without making accusations and how to own their issues rather than trying to force them on others.

Recently, a mum wanted to go straight from school pick-up to the supermarket. Her eight-year-old was shattered and desperately didn't want to go.

She noticed that he was copying her use of language. Instead of saying, "It's not fair, I don't want to go, I want to go home instead," he said, "It feels unfair, I'm so tired and I just don't have the energy for shopping, I'd have really loved to go home." The way they communicate is strongly influenced by the way we speak to them. His disappointment was easy to hear. As it happened, his elder brother was at home, so, much as she didn't want the detour, the mum felt inclined to do it because he'd given her a choice. When they pressurise us and complain, we want to dig our heels in.

WHOSE MONKEY?

So, in review, when the problem is theirs, we hunt the feeling and listen to their needs and when the problem is ours we share our feelings and express our needs through using the word 'I'. Have you heard the expression 'Not my circus, not my monkeys'? When deciding on a response it's important to know whose problem is whose – or whose monkey is whose.

It's tempting to think that when our child is being rude, running late, hasn't unloaded the dishwasher, is on their phone too much or not eating what you've cooked, that they've got the problem. However, it's actually your problem! In terms of unmet needs, they're not suffering, you are. In fact, they're just fine about all those things. Hunting for the feeling or listening to their needs

"If you get in the pit with them, soon you won't know who the smell's coming from."
- Danny Silk

will be lost on them in these cases, because each issue is well and truly *not their monkey*.

Any of the previous examples might be issues that you'd like them to take responsibility for, but in the first instance, the unmet needs are yours. You may be frustrated that you're not being spoken to politely; you've been left to unload the dishwasher; you could be annoyed about their phone useage and the wasted food, all for good reasons. It's so tempting to think of these things as your child's problems and want to shift the frustration on to them so that they respond. But in terms of looking for an effective response, it's important to know that when it's your monkey, using the word 'I' is far less likely to lead to conflict.

By the same token, our children will try to shift their frustrations on to us. If they can make us feel their problems are our problems, they can be more successful in altering the outcomes. When they don't want to have a bath, put away their toys, go to Uncle David's party, do their homework or miss the bowling gathering, or find that they've run out of tops because they didn't bring their laundry down, it's well and truly *their monkey*. And when it's their monkey, it's time to hunt the feeling and hear the need.

Dr Gordon Thomas was a pioneer of non-conflict communication in the 1950s. In fact he got a Nobel nomination for it. Most books or articles on communication can be linked back to his discoveries about how to resolve conflict:

identifying who has the unmet need and then responding accordingly.

UNMET NEED	RESPONSE
The other person's unmet need (child, spouse, colleague, neighbour...)	Empathy
My unmet need	Own the feeling ("I feel...")

He noted that you acquire more influence with young people when you give up using your power to control them and, in fact, that the more you try to control people the less influence you have on them. We have a lot to thank him for! We have found that *hunting the feeling* means that our children own their problems and can invite your help, rather than tipping their problems on you and waiting for a reaction. *Expressing the feeling* means that you own your problems and can invite their help.

As our children get older and their issues have greater consequences, it's important for them to have matured in solving and taking responsibility for their problems. If we can help them to identify when the problem is theirs, we will be less inclined to jump in and try to control their situations. Then we are free to support them in finding their solutions and making their own choices.

IN A NUTSHELL
SURVIVING CONFLICT

- Just because conflict is uncomfortable, doesn't mean it should be avoided at all costs
- There are ways to resolve conflict healthily
- If we avoid conflict, we will send our children out into the world with avoidance, rather than peace-making strategies
- The home years give us opportunities to grow their skills of listening and expressing themselves
- Making peace doesn't mean agreeing; it means accepting that someone has a different perspective
- Resolving conflict can feel messy
- Relationships that overcome differences are richer than those that avoid differences
- If we can identify whose problem it is, and either listen or invite their help, they will learn to express themselves calmly and take responsibility
- We have more influence when we give up trying to control

CHAPTER NINE – SIBLING CLASHES

Gloves on

Some gardeners subscribe to the idea that plants have got to 'fight it out amongst themselves'. They are refering to areas of the garden that need to work themselves out by jostling for the best spot. Morag explained that it doesn't always work with the more vigorous plants as they will eventually outcompete their rivals to the detriment of the weaker plant. She explained that that there are times for a gardener to step in if a plant is getting too 'bossy' and that the gardener may have to do some pruning or move a plant to a better place where it can flourish.

This reminded me of the many sibling clashes that I have heard over the years. There have been times to get into the thick of it and umpire, but also, there have been times to stand back and let the children work it out for themselves. I haven't always got that right!

Stepping back

Sibling conflict can be healthy. That might sound bonkers, but if we can teach our children to resolve their differences, they'll acquire skills and peacemaking strategies at home to take on into life.

The first thing I'd say about sibling conflict is that I wish I'd jumped in a bit less over the years. The sound of children fighting is so grating, it makes us want to get in the ring and umpire. We so desperately want harmony in the home and we know that our input could restore peace. But is it really peace? I can remember one occasion when a mother went marching up to her squabbling children in the park and forced them to apologise to each other and walked away delighted that peace had been restored. That's not making peace, it's faking peace. Nothing's been restored, it's just been controlled. I'm sure I have faked peace in my time.

A better way forward is to teach siblings the tools they need in order to resolve their own conflicts. But first, let them know the rules of play in your home. Every home will be different, but here are some examples:
- No labeling (e.g. "You're an idiot").
- No comparing.
- No boasting.
- No physical resolving.

- If the argument is ruining the peace for the rest of the family, leave the room.
- Just because it's true, doesn't mean it needed saying.

Some classic sibling complaints might include: "He hit me"; "She took my toy"; "He tripped me up"; "I had it first"; she said, he did... As children get older, they still like you to see their side. In fact, I'm not sure we ever grow out of that desire for someone to understand why we feel aggrieved.

Some tempting responses are:
- *"You two are always arguing."*
- *"I can't comment because I wasn't watching."*
- *"You shouldn't have called him a..."*
- *"I'm not surprised this has ended in tears."*

Empathy is a good starting point:
- *"I'm so sorry you're upset."*
- *"That must feel unfair."*
- *"I'm sorry you're hurt."*

I'm not a neurologist, but when my children's issues have been met with empathy I can virtually see their Amygdala shrink from being a large, frothing, angry bear to a small, more peaceful, slightly cross, domestic kitten.

"An enemy is someone whose story you have not heard." - Old Jewish saying

Once you've had a chance to express your empathy, encourage the aggrieved child (the one whose monkey it is), to express their feeling to the other sibling.

For example, if he's complaining that he was pushed, encourage him to let his sibling know how being pushed makes him feel. Try to have the same prompt each time, for example, "Share with him/her how you feel." Over time they will learn to express their needs rather than accusing:

- *"I get cross when things are taken from me."*
- *"It upsets me when I'm called names."*

Then encourage them to add their need

- *"Please could you ask me when you want something."*
- *"Please be kind with your words."*

It's not always realistic (or helpful) to get to the bottom of each problem, so much is about each person's perspective.

Effective communication is 20 per cent fact and 80 per cent how you feel about the fact.

As they get older, they will pick up the non-accusatory narrative and learn to be more respectful through the teen years:

- *"I don't like finding that my things have been borrowed without being asked first."* Then, *"Please ask me before taking stuff from my room."*
- *"I was hoping there would be some biscuits left when I got home."* Then, *"Next time please could you leave some for me."*

In the early days of using this method, you may need to support them through it. It's much easier to back children up when accusations aren't flying around. Once they get the hang of it, you can give them space to resolve their own issues.

If they want to resolve, but they're too wound up, you can offer to help. "It looks as though you two have a difficult issue. I'm happy to help when everyone's calmer."

Sometimes, when they're in no mood to resolve and it's really wearing you thin, then I'm afraid it's your monkey. "I'm finding this conflict upsetting, I need it to be taken upstairs/outside."

"The single biggest problem in communication is the illusion that it has taken place."

- George Bernard Shaw, playwright

Mediation

With both of these statements, they will learn that their arguments don't get you to drop what you're doing and give them your full attention. In fact, if they're in a season of fighting with each other it is possible to give them a consequence. Let them know how draining it is for you and that you'll need them to do a few chores because you've run out of energy.

Two of our children went through a period of seemingly constant bickering which interfered with everyone's peace and was draining. After a few rounds of cleaning the bathroom, they began to check themselves before going into battle. We were still open to listening and giving them a chance to talk about their differences, but it reduced the petty fighting.

Children respond differently to conflict; quite often one will come and chat about it and the other will process internally. When they've calmed down, it's constructive to try to chat to each of them, then empathise and help them to think about a way forward:

- "It sounds like you've had a tough time."
- "What are you thinking you'll do next?"
- "What do you think the outcome of that would be?"
- "I'm sorry you two are having a hard time."

Sometimes, when they're battle weary, our children's conflicts need a bit of informal mediation. Under the age of four, it's hard to have a reasoned conversation with them about their arguments, but from as young as four or five they can be receptive and even surprise us with suggestions of how to reconcile.

If mediation is needed, let them know that they can have some breathing space and that you're all going to come back and chat about the issue. That reinforces the message that you'll respond in your time, rather than react to their noise. Choose a time when you can sit with them. Let them know that you'd like to get together to hear both of their perspectives. They're far more likely to come willingly if they know you're coming to hear them rather that tell them off.

Allow them to have a few minutes each to speak uninterrupted about what's upset them (the amount of minutes will depend on their age). It takes a few experiences before they get the hang of this. Listening without interrupting is hard enough for an adult, let alone an aggrieved child. However, as long as they know that you're just listening to each point of view, not accepting everything as fact, and that they will get their go, they'll wait for their turn.

BASIC NEUROSCIENCE

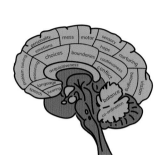

HEAD FIRST

Some people see everything with their head first, before they move on to their feelings. Children with this personality type are logical and rational and their arguments will always concentrate on the facts. "He hit me first. My punch wasn't that hard. It was my ball."
This child is often quite articulate and finds it easier to argue without getting emotional. They sometimes feel they're more competent than the child who uses their heart first because the brain is doing the work in that scenario. It doesn't mean they don't have emotions – they're just able to compartmentalise more easily. It's often the case that the facts (as they see them) feel more urgent than harmony for this person.

HEART FIRST

Other people see everything with their heart first, before they move to logical ground. They won't just be physically hurt by being hit; they'll be emotionally bruised and trying to process it. Their feelings will be raw and more important than the facts. If they feel they're being railroaded by the person arguing from the head, they can either shut down or point out weaknesses in their opponent's character. Or they may just concede because they prioritise harmony over truth, but the unresolved conflict gets trapped. A parent can help the head-first thinker to consider what it felt like to the heart-first thinker and vice versa.

Growing character

Children may get to the end of listening and neither party wants to give an inch. They're quite within their rights to hang on to their perspective. The purpose here is not to persuade them to apologise, it is to come away having been listened to – they may process differently as a result. If the aim in your home is to be respectful to one another, then hearing each other is a helpful habit to teach them.

We've been amazed by the understanding our children have developed in these times together. It's interesting to watch them as they begin to engage with the other child's feelings. We've often heard them say, "I hadn't realised that," or they've expressed an understanding that they didn't have before. Sometimes there have been external factors weighing in, which the other party wasn't aware of. At the end, you can ask if anyone feels an apology is a good idea. This way they make the decision for themselves, which is so much more effective than a forced 'sorry'. Sometimes they've even ended by saying something kind and uplifting.

This process is time-consuming and you may be wondering how realistic it is. I hope it encourages you to know that once you've given your children the skills and invested some time into a few different scenarios, they begin to either give up the argument, rather than go through the listening process, or learn to listen to each other without your intervention. I can remember the day that two of our children took themselves off to the lounge together after a fallout to sit and listen to each other. I was absolutely stunned and it felt like a victorious moment.

Mediating can seem a little intense at first. It's a bit like when you get a new filling from the dentist – it can feel like an enormous carbuncle in your mouth, but then, without actually changing size at all, the new shape in your mouth feels less and less obvious, until it feels completely normal. It's not, of course, it's just a new normal. When new habits get hard-wired they become a natural part of family life. A new normal. And so it is with resolving conflict.

A culture of respect, like all cultures, takes time to establish and grow. As parents, we can help our children by using conflict as a learning opportunity and we can also model it for them by resolving our arguments with our partner and apologising to each other in front of our children.

They won't always resolve all their issues, in fact they probably won't resolve most of them. But if the culture in your home is to listen, respect, have empathy and try to resolve, then conflict will be developmental and what they learn at home will positively impact all their relationships.

_____

If you don't own your stuff, you'll spend the rest of your life feeling let down by everyone

IN A NUTSHELL
SIBLING CLASHES

- Sibling clashes can be productive
- Sometimes we need to step in, sometimes we need to step back
- Make peace, don't fake peace
- Let them know the 'rules of play' in your home
- Empathise!
- Help them to express their feelings, not make accusations
- Don't let their arguments win your attention
- Practise mediation
- Develop a culture of respect
- Expect mediating to be time-consuming at first

The Power of Gratitude

Gratitude is a difficult thing to teach. It's really not the same as learning to say 'please' and 'thank you', valuable as that is. Gratitude is an attitude.

Whether our children own plenty or little, their level of contentedness will be impacted by their level of gratitude. Gratitude isn't about what you have or don't have. It's about whether you're grateful for what you do have.

Model it. Expressing gratitude to our children is influential. It encourages them to speak about what they feel grateful for. Letting them know about the little or big things we're thankful for establishes a culture in the home of sharing thankfulness.

- *"I'm thrilled that shop was able to mend my bike."*
- *"I love these flowers that Sue dropped off today."*
- *"I'm so excited about the new table."*
- *"Wasn't it kind of Jo to lend us this game?"*

Encourage it. At the end of each day or over dinner we can ask our children to share three things they feel grateful for. If they can't think of any then it's probably a sure sign that this is an area that needs a little development. There's so much to be grateful for.

A few years ago, I began writing down 'four things I loved about yesterday' in a little book I keep by my bed. It never takes more than a minute to fill it in. What I didn't know when I started was how those books (I have two now) would bless me in years to come. I find that I sometimes forget the details of life and wish I could do it all over again, but my little books have become ledgers of happy moments that I love to read.

- Noises of a young family waking
- Little boy breaths on my pillow
- Perseverance at the piano
- Children catching bubbles
- A friend at the door
- Swimming lengths – peace!
- Warm afternoon
- Little feet barely making it to the end of the chair
- Frosty day
- A hopeful dog watching us decorate cakes

All that before mindfulness became a buzzword!

DELAY GRATIFICATION

If our children receive everything they want and need, they are more likely to become entitled than grateful. Psychology studies have shown that 'high-delay' children have fewer behavioural problems and end up performing better academically. Conversely children who have trouble delaying gratification were more prone to addiction. Asking them to financially contribute to things they want also earns them a sense of reward.

Teaching our children to stretch their ability to wait for pleasures develops not only patience, but also their appreciation for things they have waited for. In other words, gratitude.

People who are grateful have higher levels of satisfaction, self-esteem and optimism

CHAPTER TEN – SOCIAL MEDIA

Garden Maintenance

A well-maintained garden is a healthy garden. Only a garden that is maintained produces edible fruits and vegetables as well as beautiful flowers. Maintaining the garden also improves the desirability of the property. A neglected garden produces weeds and fat garden pests. We can't neglect our parental duties if we want our children to flourish, so it is important that we are all aware of the hazards, as well as the benefits, of social media.

Mental health

In this final chapter, I thought it would be helpful to review the chapters by taking one specific issue and using it as a working example of all the parenting skills and tools covered throughout the book. I've chosen social media.

I love social media; it's here to stay and we need to embrace it. But we also need to understand the impact it is having on young people so we can help our children to self-regulate.

I work alongside a counsellor, Caroline Kelly, who counsels children and teenagers. She was recently invited to a primary school by a distressed headteacher to help with an epidemic of self-harming among ten-year-olds. She discovered that whilst their parents had been monitoring their children's Instagram accounts, they were unaware of their secret alternative accounts where they were communicating with strangers who promoted self-harming and suicide. Caroline has many examples from her working experience of social media having had unhealthy influences and detrimental effects on young people's mental health. She believes it's not coincidental that the rise in anxiety, mental health issues and self-harming among children and teenagers followed the explosion of social media around 2010.

We are living in a season where social media is widely available, yet its full impact on mental health is relatively unresearched. Over 200 years ago there were theories emerging about tobacco having a negative impact on health, but it wasn't until 1955 that major studies concluded the fact.

It's likely that in another decade there will be enough evidence to show the link between social media and mental health issues. The government may then begin to put regulations in place. In the meantime, our children are that research and parents can feel that they're in the dark.

Not everyone will suffer with mental health issues because of social media, just as not everyone who uses alcohol and even binge drinks will become an alcoholic. But there are many families whose children will be negatively impacted by social media and many that already are. It's certainly addictive and in a recent survey by *Young Mind Matters* a staggering 81 per cent of parents blamed social media for making their adolescents more vulnerable to mental health problems. In fact, the number of young people seeking counselling is higher than ever and teenage suicides are at their highest in fourteen years in the UK, at four cases per week (Data ONS).

Impulsive

The recent developments in neuroscience have given us helpful insights into how the adolescent brain works. We know (see page 54), that the PreFrontal Cortex doesn't fully develop until a person is in their mid-twenties. Its functions include insight, judgement, impulse control, planning, problem solving and emotional reasoning. Without having matured in these functions, the adolescent brain resorts to impulsive choices rather than reflection and research. An adolescent's decisions are largely based on rewards and emotions.

Their developing brain is often drawn towards the reward without thinking about the consequences. No wonder teenagers love the edgy stuff: free running, jumping off high cliffs, bombing down-hill on their bikes, not thinking about the possibility of a broken leg. Whilst impetuous decisions and youthful adventure is an important part of growing up, without the back-up cognitive strength of the PreFrontal Cortex, young people sometimes make poor decisions.

Linking this to social media, the impulsivity of a young mind (or an older one!) can lead to posting or sending on social media without always reflecting on the potential consequences, which causes problems, hurts and even disasters through both private and public posts. The experience of being hurt, left out or bullied used to only happen in school or public settings, but now these experiences can follow children and teenagers into their bedrooms.

Each family makes its own decisions about the appropriate age for social media, but it's worth knowing the legal age requirement for each different app. It's also important to consider the cognitive limitations of a child under thirteen when giving them access.

Caroline frequently sees the characteristics of addiction among the teenagers she works with, such as irritability, aggression, poor concentration, emotional instability, depression, anxiety and difficulty sleeping to name a few.

Some teenagers don't cope without their phone, it's with them day and night. Attempts by their parents to regulate their exposure end in anger, irritation and turmoil and many young people admit they are addicted to their phones. In a recent client survey of teenagers, they *all* admitted that they wished mobile phones and social media had never been invented.

BASIC NEUROSCIENCE

DOPAMINE

We are motivated to satisfy our needs and desires due to a neurotransmitter in the brain called dopamine. This ensures we pursue our primal needs for food, shelter and warmth and it can also drive us to gratify the urge for sex, sugar, alcohol or drugs. It could equally trigger us to satisfy the desire for the comfort of affection or even social affirmation (through personal interaction or social media). Dopamine can also propel us to chase thrills from experiences like extreme sports or gambling.

It has been more recently discovered that dopamine isn't just associated with satisfaction, but is also related to the anticipation of satisfaction – the thrill of the chase. Generally, the chase will come to a natural end as we get warm, full, satisfied, exhausted or drunk, depending on what we are were seeking. But there is a toxic combination now available to our children and teenagers: the increased dopamine that the adolescent brain experiences together with the inexhaustible opportunities of digital technology.

Dopamine can facilitate the potentially endless cycle of chasing and attaining on the internet. It's no wonder many more parents are reporting seeing the symptoms of screen addiction in their adolescents, such as:

AGITATION, ANXIETY, MANIA, HYPERACTIVITY, INABILITY TO CONCENTRATE, INSOMNIA AND DEPRESSION.

Addiction

Adam Alters, psychologist, argues that addiction was always the intention of social media. He cites in his book, *The Rise of Addictive Technology And The Business Of Keeping Us Hooked*, that insiders knew that the devices, apps, social media platforms and experiences they were creating had the capacity of "doling out dopamine hits like tiny bits of cocaine". This was done in the knowledge that the longer we spend on social media sites, the more advertising revenue could be generated.

Social media, news, gaming and dating sites have no stopping-queues. Gone are the days when a TV episode was over and we waited a week for the next one. There are no natural endings. I know myself that one peek at the BBC news site can lead to endless mining for more information, just as the designers intended.

It's interesting to note that Steve Jobs admitted to a journalist, two years after the iPad had been launched, that his children still weren't allowed access. Perhaps his insight was similar to employees of tech giants Google, Apple and Yahoo, many of whom also protect their children by sending them to schools where tech is banned, such as the Waldorf School in Silicon Valley. It's an open secret that we, the users, are in fact the product; we're data information; advertising fodder. Yet, there are so many advantages to having all these free applications at our finger tips. Could there really be any harm?

Caroline's work has led her to understand the debilitating impact of anxiety on young minds. We've looked at the body's fight or flight reactor (see page 54) and how it responds when we are fearful, which is vital for survival in the face of danger. However, the same neurological process can trigger when posting on a story line or sending an image. As soon as a child or teen has sent something, they've lost control. Their inability to retract a post they regret; their lack of certainty over other people's responses; their sense of rejection when they are blocked by a 'friend' or when they see on FaceBook or SnapMap that they're not invited to an event, can trigger fear. These experiences can come at them in a constant stream.

Some stress is perfectly normal. Children and adolescents have enough of that with school work, family issues and making sense of the world around them. However, when the mind is constantly stressed, it leads to the over-production of cortisol which is detrimental to health.

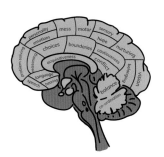

CORTISOL

Cortisol is a hormone produced by the body to help us respond to threatening situations. It triggers our bodies to flood our muscles with glucose, producing energy for us to rise up and fight...or run away! It's potentially life saving. But it is intended for high stress moments, not as a way of life, because in those stressful moments, when the body prepares for response, other things become inhibited such as our immune system, digestive system and even our physical growth.

None of these things are needed for that short stint whilst you're on red alert. Then when the panic is over our bodies can return to normal. We can take a deeeeeep breath, and our inhibited systems can reactivate. But if we remain stressed for long periods of time, it takes its toll on our heart, digestive system and mental wellbeing. This leaves us susceptible to burnout, depression and ill health. Studies have shown that the more exposure a child or teenager has to social media, the higher their cortisol levels. But in order to relieve stress, they often turn back to the internet for social reassurance to counter those feelings of stress. And the cycle begins. Sometimes to the point of addiction...

There are some studies now available that show the alarming levels of night-disruption children and teenagers experience, as well as the number of times their phones get tapped during the day and the hours of exposure. But Caroline wouldn't need any of this evidence as she has daily confirmation that young people are not giving their brains a chance to switch off and she is seeing the impact of that on their concentration, relationships, work, sleep and general wellbeing.

This all indicates that they need a little help to make healthy choices.

The good news is that, as parents, we have the ability to influence our children whilst their brain's PreFrontal lobe is still under construction.

Parenting well

Trying to regulate our children's exposure to social media can feel overwhelming. One of the reasons is that our kids are ahead of us here. Even if you've reached great heights in the tech world, you're still considered a visitor to cyber-world, whereas our children are considered the natives. The kids have become the hosts; the parents, grand parents, teachers and carers are playing catch-up.

It's tempting to stick our heads in the sand and hope our children will survive it all, or alternatively to alienate them from the dangers of their own world through control and force. However, there is another option: we can find compromises that enable us to protect the natives and train them, whilst staying in good relationships with them.

PLANNING

The home years are our children's training ground for their adult life and the place where they develop their muscle of self-control. They will face far more temptations than any other generation before them. If we avoid all the dangers out there, we miss the chance to strengthen our children to navigate their way through the adulthood that's waiting for them. But developing muscle takes time, consistency, commitment and a plan. So, let's look at how to do that, whether you're at the stage where your children are having a regular iPaddy, or you're trying to retrieve your teenager's face from their mobile phone.

Two-way agreement

When the time comes for your child to have access to social media, you could consider making a contract with them. You would have to sign one yourself before a provider will give you a phone, so by the same token, it's helpful to offer your children a two-way contract. This can be done verbally or even in writing. Either way, it helps children to have a clear understanding of your boundaries (see Chapter Six).

If your child already has access to a phone or social media, it isn't too late to consider establishing some boundaries in the form of a contract (after all, you're probably paying their phone bill). It's not easy to retrace steps, however, we would think nothing of taking a knife out of a toddler's hand or pulling a small child back if they headed for the road. We have that same duty to protect them when they're older. They may resist us more, but our boundaries still make them feel safe and cared for and there are ways to revisit the boundaries without too much damage. But, before you think about what might be in the two-way agreement, it's worth listening to what they have to say first. After all, they're reporting directly from the front line.

LISTENING

By listening to their views on technology and personal tech, you will be taking the issue from between you, where it is a potential point of conflict, and putting it in front of you both (see Chapter Eight).

A helpful start is to ask your child what they think the pros and cons are and challenge them to write down a few of each, whilst you do the same. One parent did this recently and was encouraged by some of the points her child made. Her daughter's list included, 'Media sites don't have children's interests at heart.' Her daughter will be far more likely to engage with this as a fact now it's come from her, rather than told to her. Another child cited that it helped his social confidence, which is a great conversation to have with him.

I don't know what your children might say, but understanding is such a good way to enter into any agreement where they have to abide by some boundaries. It makes them feel that their perspective has been considered.

Boundaries

The boundaries will differ from home to home. Here are some suggestions you may like to consider. Some of them may be familiar already.

TIME LIMITS

It's a good idea to separate gaming time from social media time and TV time (or equivalent). That way, you and your child have a clear understanding of how much time they spend communicating with the outside world as opposed to watching a programme or playing games.

WHEN

I know some parents allow their kids to have screen-time as an incentive to get ready for school and they find that works for them. We found that ours started getting up too early, motivated by screens; the same can happen on the weekend. So your boundaries might depend on whether you think they are negatively affected by the incentive of screen-time. If they are, you might also consider not permitting screen-time on weekends before a set time.

MONITORING TIME

Once you've considered an age-appropriate screen-time allowance, it's good for them to be responsible for it. If they're unable to show that they're timing themselves, a logical consequence would be to lose it for a day or a set period. After all, if they can use an electronic device, they should also be adept at finding the timing facility on it. That way they learn to be accountable.

PHONES

The 'right' age to have a mobile phone is up for conjecture, but armed with all of Caroline's experience, it's worth considering whether you could wait until senior school. However, each family will have their own views and these are only suggestions based on research and experience.

BREAKS

We ask our pre-Sixth Form kids to hand their phones in when they get back from school and they get them back after dinner, if homework is done. That way they get a breather from that incessant online world and we find they engage more with family life. Similarly, we have a tech amnesty on Sunday afternoons, which they also manage to survive. In an honest moment, they'll even admit to enjoying it.

PLATFORMS

Thirteen is the recommended age for social media and we've found that feels about right. Most platforms will ask for the applicant's age and disallow under-age applications. However, some don't ask their age and there are certainly no checks in place to see if the applicant is giving the correct age. (This is an area the government could fight for!)

Once our children are allowed social media, we let them loose on *Facebook* or *Instagram*. *SnapChat* has caused so many difficulties for young people, it makes sense to let them grow into that one! Our latest newcomer chose *Instagram*. You can follow or friend them on their new app.

HELPING THEM TO MAKE CHOICES

Some apps are not permitted in our home. It's hard for you to track them all as over 5,000 new apps become available every day. However, there are some common ones which you may feel are worth avoiding. I'll list a couple of sites that are currently causing difficulties for young people and you can visit Caroline and my website for updates (www.notonthebackfoot.com).

Yellow is a teenage version of *Tinder*; swipe left or right to connect with new 'friends'. We avoid this one because we feel social media should be a place to connect with friends already made, not the other way around. *Yellow* is notorious for being rife with predators pressurising young people to expose themselves.

Omegle is a site where visitors can 'make friends with strangers' via webcam and it's renowned for its pornographic material, which they can record. I was recently made aware of an issue in a school where ten-year-olds were sending other children in their class pornographic videos found on *Omegle*. Apart from the mayhem it caused at the school and the detrimental effect on one child in particular, the school had to involve the police because it is a criminal offence for minors to be in possession of pornographic material.

Whisper is another platform to be cautious about. It's a place for anonymous confessions: not a healthy way to process emotions!

When they do move onto *Snapchat*, you can insist on 'ghost' mode to avoid your children being tracked by advertisers, as they go from shop to eatery to friend's houses leaving a trail of data. Also, be aware of the strange allure of streaks. If they have *Snaphat* they can attain streaks by posting to the same person, on a daily basis. The more streaks you have, the more popular you feel you are.

Personal problems require personal solutions, not social attention

MONITORING CONTENT

Some parents choose to have open access to their children's tech and this can be an effective way to see some of what they've been sending and viewing. However, it's far from fool-proof.

Our preference is to go through their media with them from time to time. Can you remember during childhood when you were watching a movie with your parents and then a love-scene came on? It was far more cringey when parents were present. By the same token, the material that looks completely innocuous to a child when they're alone, can suddenly be seen in a totally different light when showing it to Mum or Dad. They'll often volunteer to make changes and that can also open conversations about online values.

Part of our agreement with our teens is that we can spot check their phones. They don't love it, but they do prefer that method to us rifling through their phones when they're not present.

This method is not foolproof either, but it feels more relational. They get the opportunity to explain why certain things are in there and we find that they often choose to make changes before we've suggested it as we go through it together.

I was amused recently to see so many pictures of duvets, feet and blankets among one of our children's photos. The reason was 'streaks'. If you had to send a photo on a daily basis to everyone you knew and you were permitted to have your phone by your bed, I guess you might well grab it first thing in the morning and take a photo of the nearest thing. Be aware that there are vaults which have been created to hide pictures and information. Some of them are created to look like innocent music apps or even a calculator app! **(updates on www.notonthebackfoot.com)**

Protecting their rest

To the mild frustration of our older teenagers, we do expect them all to return their phone to the chargers in the kitchen half an hour before bedtime. You could opt for turning the Wi-Fi off instead, if you can remember. Screen light affects sleep cycles, so it's also advisable to get them to set the blue light filter to come on automatically an hour before bed-time.

It's also helpful to ask them to turn off their notifications so that the little pings and lights don't set their dopamine foraging. One of the most common reasons parents give for letting

"I thought my boundaries were foolproof when I said, 'No food in the lounge and no screens in the kitchen.' " - Parent

their children keep their phones in their rooms at night is that they use it as an alarm clock. You'll be pleased to hear they are now available as separate devices.

Occasionally I'll be in the kitchen late at night or in the wee hours and the notifications are coming through at high speed. Young people are active throughout the night if permitted. I don't think most children would be able to resist all that communication if they had their phone by their beds. This is an area where we need to be brave with our boundaries if we want them to get the rest and relief they need from the communicating world.

I usually find that where parents report disconnection, difficulty communicating with their teenager or the sense of alienation from them or their inner world, it is rare to find that they've put boundaries around phones, bedtimes and bedrooms.

Some might say that *all* teenagers will disconnect, stop communicating or go through some teenage tunnel. I'd say that's absolute twaddle. It's a lie we've been fed. Our teenagers will develop independence but they don't need to be disconnected from us. I know of many families, including our own, where connection isn't lost through those years.

Safeguards

There are some controls you can put on yours and your childrens' technology, which will enable you to monitor, block and track their usage from your own device. However, there are no electronic safeguards that substitute for good parental modelling, supervision and guidance.

Your part of the deal

A contract is two-sided. One of the most effective ways of making an impression on our children is by modelling. What we 'do' often makes a greater impression than what we 'say'. There have been some interesting newspaper articles about children feeling powerless in home situations when their parents are on their devices:

- *"Dad doesn't listen to me when he's on his phone."*
- *"Sometimes I talk to Mum and she doesn't answer."*
- *"It makes me feel like they don't care."*

That's you and me! Technology has revolutionised our world and it can be hard to put down without dropping spinning plates. But whether we're booking a holiday, transferring money, accepting an invitation (often on our child's behalf), buying a gift or flipping through news or social media, it all looks the same to our children.

"Be the change you want to see in the world." - Mahatma Gandhi

Do you ever answer your phone in the middle of a conversation with your children? Do you look at it during dinner? Or check it at breakfast time? You could offer to show self-control in these areas. You could also offer to put safeguards on your phone that track your usage to help you gauge how much you are using your phone.

One mum moved all her social media to the end of her home-screen apps so that she had to swipe a few times before accessing it, which reduced her use of social media. Another parent took WhatsApp off their notifications and many parents stop their phone from buzzing and beeping when texts and notifications come in.

When we have limitations we agree to, we can model self-control and let them know when we find it difficult. It's helpful for them to see that we don't abandon self-control just because it isn't easy. We can also tell them what we're doing when we are on our phones. Sometimes it's useful for them to know you're not in a WhatsApp volley with a friend but, in-fact, putting money on their school lunch account.

Consequences

As our children get older, one thing is for sure; they will have a different perspective from us about how much social media is appropriate for them. We can set boundaries and let them know our expectations or we can just complain about their over-usage: "I can't get that flipping thing out of her hand." "Why doesn't he ever put that thing down?" are among many complaints I often hear and ones that parents admit to saying in ranting moments. The problem is that nagging and complaining is not empowered. It is disempowered and reactive.

We know from Chapter Six that boundaries are not much use unless they're enforceable. Whatever consequences you decide upon, it's important to be sure that they're directly related to the issue. If I don't fill the car with petrol, it will come to a grinding halt somewhere inconvenient; nobody will stop my pocket money or put me to bed early.

It's so easy to use our children's tech as a punishment for just about everything. I was standing next to a mum recently and she spotted her son sneaking another biscuit. She immediately said, "If you eat that, you won't get your phone for the rest of the day." I can see the temptation. It hits where it hurts, but, with respect, it isn't relevant and it's confusing for them. If our response has nothing to do with the poor choice, it's not a consequence, it's a punishment. If they've stolen biscuits from the biscuit tin, let the consequences be food-related. If they've left their belongings around, let the consequence be chore-related. That way, your boundaries and consequences around tech are much clearer for them to understand.

One consequence that we use for mobile phones is, for example, if their phone is found in their bedroom after the curfew, they lose it for a week the first time and then a month.

(Of course, there are a myriad of ways they can access social media without actually having their phone – old phones, iPads, a friend's computer, but it's been an effective consequence none the less.)

Conflict

What do we do when they pour their wrath on us because they're walking in a well-chosen consequence of a poor choice they've made?

We can be quite sure they won't always be in agreement with our wonderful parenting ideas. I remember one particular occasion when our eight-year-old was furious with me for doling out a consequence. When my husband came home that evening, my son asked to see him in the bedroom. "About that woman you married," he began, "Is that your final choice?" He was disappointed, at that time, to find that I was

a permanent fixture. But, I'm looking forward to cheekily reminding him of that quote on his wedding day!

As uncomfortable as it is to be in conflict with our children, it is possible to be strong and gentle at the same time. If our consequences are fair and well thought through, we don't have to get angry. In fact, our first response can be empathy.

Empathy defuses. If they're finding it hard to be the only child in the universe who's not allowed to take their phone to bed, you can empathise.

When our fourteen-year-old had his phone taken away for a month, he was in a big strop the next morning. I didn't need to get annoyed with him, or lecture him, the consequence was doing the teaching. That left me free to say, "I realise this must be hard for you. I'm sorry you're finding it difficult."

Of course, I was tempted to say, "I warned you!" But I restrained on this occasion. It's okay for them to be annoyed. They're allowed to have feelings – particularly when they're detoxing!

REJECTION

They're not rejecting us, they're rejecting our boundaries. It's their job. If we can't bear to lose their approval because we're seeking their

friendship, then we're not parenting. We're just looking to meet our own relational needs. They need us to be courageous and gentle parents, not 'bezzys'. As one parent said to me recently, "The pain of rejection is nothing to the pain of regret."

BOOST THEM
Each year our children get a little older and a little more independent and we can be fooled into thinking they need us less. It's not true. The truth is they think they need us less. They seem to put a far higher value on time with their friends (or people they've 'friended'), but actually, they thrive on our attention.

After food and shelter, our three most basic human needs for emotional survival are: Significance, acceptance and belonging. That's what snap, ping, chat, pose is all about - make me feel special, accept me and let me belong.

It is important for our children to feel they fit into social groups and belong in various places. They will actively chase this affirmation from others, sometimes to the point of addiction. But it is our words, our touch and our time that deeply nurtures them. We've learned that the brain of the tween or teen hasn't fully developed, so they will tend to opt for what they want rather than what they need.

In this fast-moving world, it can be hard to make time for each of our children. I don't know how easy that's been for you over the last week or month: time alone with one child, such as a date at a coffee shop; listening empathetically or remembering to give them lots of hugs and encouraging words. I know those things can go out of the window quite quickly when I get over-busy. All these activities along with spending family time together through meals, walks and games build trust and identity. They're powerful. They release oxytocin (see page 61), which is a much-needed antidote to the stress and challenges in their lives.

Antidotes

There isn't actually a magic button, but it is true that our children will get an enhanced dopamine release in early adolescence, which peaks midway through and which will tempt them to be drawn to thrills and excitement. A common view is to see adolescence as a stage to get over. If we do that, we're missing a trick. What we cultivate in those years will shape the rest of their lives. Looking for new adventures and stepping out socially are part of their development. If we prevent or ignore these natural steps, they'll miss out – and we might too.

Putting some edgy thrills into their lives is a way to engage with their natural instincts, which builds relationship. If their only way to get thrills is online, they will become more dependent on their devices and be susceptible to the antisocial and negative side-effects.

Giving them our time, acceptance, inclusion and with a side-serving of adventure meets some of their deepest needs for connection, which can reduce their motivation to chase internet affirmation. Building trust helps us to communicate openly with them and influence them as they navigate the wonderful, captivating, inspiring yet noisy, clamoring online world.

As one of the last generations who will remember life before technology, we know the contrast of a world without it, so it's hard not to be fearful about this new world they are a part of. The concepts in these pages will stand the test of time, whether you're facing age-old battles or ones we haven't heard of yet.

We may not be natives of cyber world, but our children are still natives of our world and their basic needs haven't changed since time began. Giving them a strong sense of belonging, as well as empathetically listening to them and offering them freedom to make good and poor choices, gives them a healthy culture to grow up in. Adding well thought-through boundaries,

backed up by consequences helps us to stay calm, empowered and even empathetic in the face of conflict. If we do this in a culture of love, affection and connected relationship with a side-serving of adventure, we have a strong chance of launching unique, empowered, relational, confident, secure, likeable, empathetic, fun-loving adults into the world.

Children will take their values from the group they feel they most strongly belong to

The Power of Adventure

When you look back at the stories of your youth, which ones come to mind? Are they the ones that pushed the norms, felt a bit edgy, required risk?

We're all wired to stretch past our comfort zones and feel the heady rush of dopamine (see Page 168) urging us to bash down the confining walls of safety and embrace a bit of danger. The trouble is, nowadays we can do all that from an armchair. For our children, much of gaming is heroic stuff. Then, as they get older, much of what's available in cyber-world is edgy, but not necessarily in a healthy way. All that motivation for a thrill can be done without even standing up. However, in these formative years, we can show our children some more exhilarating alternatives.

The world is a great playground. When I think of adventure, it usually involves the outdoors: camping, woods, boats, bikes, compasses, stones, sticks, fires. I know some of you don't like camping (which could account for why 50 per cent of kids have never slept in a garden or field), but there are always day trips.

Adventure doesn't have to be expensive either. There are so many things you can do to inspire your children that are far cheaper than the electronic alternatives or soft play centres or trampoline lands (great as they are). I will concede that adventure is inconvenient because it requires us getting out and about, but the benefits are worth it.

SHARED EXPERIENCES

Relationships are strengthened through shared challenges. Exploring together will give your children a memory bank of shared experiences. They will learn, laugh and persevere together. Companies take their employees on outward-bound adventures because condensed experiences that involve challenges help people to understand each other, which helps them to bond. This is true of siblings too. Adventure also builds our children's confidence, develops their initiative, gives them skills and helps them to learn about themselves.

When children hit the tween and teen years, their brains are wired to crave the rush they get from chasing adventure. Drinking, drugs, casual sex and social media exploits can easily satisfy the nagging desire for an adrenaline rush. If we raise them with healthy adventures, some of their cravings will be met and that will reduce their need for online adventure, but importantly, we'll be forming good habits through these impressionable years.

They're never too young to start going on little adventures. And it's never too late to start either. Older children may drag their feet and have a sulk, but they do that at home too. We don't always need their approval for a family day out and those children that do drag their feet rarely regret the adventure by the end.

Let them whittle wood with pocket knives, make a fire and poke sticks into it, use the electric drill, go wild swimming, take torches or luminous wrist bands to the park in the dark (it only needs to be four o'clock in a British winter). Lay some blankets on the trampoline or the grass and watch the stars, even sleep outside together. We loved making a bed out of the trampoline – dog and all! Go on a treasure hunt, take a camp stove up a hill and cook breakfast, cycle down muddy hills, dam a stream, climb a peak, learn to use a compass, fly a kite, take a large rubber ring and dash down a fast-flowing river.

Show them that adventure doesn't have to be electronic or narcotic, raise them on natural substitutes. Live!

"The greatest danger in life is not taking the adventure at all. To have the objective of a life of ease is death. I think we've all got to go after our own Everest."

- Brian Blessed, actor

HARVEST

Remember the experiment with two sets of seeds that I mentioned at the beginning of the book?

If our children are given the time and nourishment they need, they will establish healthy roots and they will be able to thrive throughout their childhood and their adult life.

Nature teaches us that a well-protected acorn in nutritious soil can develop into an oak tree with roots deep and wide enough to support a tree of up to 100 foot tall.

About Me

Madeleine Stanimeros

AUTHOR, BLOGGER, CONSULTANT, SPEAKER, MUM

Madeleine lives in Cheltenham with her husband Con and their five children (well, those that are still at home) and her faithful labrador, Bella. When she's not tapping away on the keyboard by the fire, speaking or consulting, she'll be having a cuppa with a friend; enjoying the Cotswold hills with the dog; desperately trying to win card games against her kids – and mum; around a table with friends, family and food; trying a new recipe; in a pool; on a bike; in her caravan; caring for a litter of puppies; making a pizza oven; making dough whilst Con fires up the pizza oven; running a music group (in-spite of not being able to sing), or enjoying a home full of the endless trail of young people who know where to find chocolate cake in Cheltenham. Her husband would add – or on the phone again!

Madeleine is available as a speaker, consultant and writer.
Contact madeleine on *madeleinestani@icloud.com*
Website *thecourageousmumma.com*   Instagram *@madeleine_stanimeros*

Explore More

SOCIAL MEDIA SEMINARS

Want to create a safer social media experience for your children?

Keen to understand the impact of social media on the brain?

Concerned by how children are using social media and its potential pitfalls?

———————————

Madeleine is joined by school counsellor and CBT Therapist, Caroline Kelly, in offering a two-hour presentation and Q&A to answer these common questions at your school or work-place, through thier organisation, You're Not on the Back Foot.

This event will give you:

- An understanding of adolescent brain development and the impact of social media on young people's mental health.

- An outline of the potential impact of social media from a teenager's perspective as they share their personal experience by video.

- Practical strategies and examples to support you in helping children to manage social media without harming your relationship with them.

- An opportunity to share your own concerns and ask questions.

Caroline Kelly | SCHOOL COUNSELLOR & CBT THERAPIST

Caroline Kelly is a professional working with children and adolescents to support their mental health and well being. She has worked in primary and secondary schools as well as her own private practice and has a particular interest in supporting young people with anxiety, depression and addiction.

Contact carolinekelly_uk@yahoo.co.uk

Alex Chalk | MP FOR CHELTENHAM

"I highly recommend the social media presentation by You're Not On The Back Foot. Caroline's explanation of social media's impact on the developing brain is enlightening, whilst Madeleine's parental guidance is reassuring yet empowering." This is required watching for any concerned parent." Website www.alexchalk.com

FUTHER INFORMATION:

To book a social media presentation notonthebackfoot.com

All other enquiries yourenotonthebackfoot@gmail.com

BLOG

Follow **The Courageousmumma** for more stories, ideas and inspiration

www.thecourageousmumma.com

BOOK CLUB

There is a page on my website with questions and ideas to spark conversations about the different topics within the book.

PARENTING COURSE

If you would like to use this book as a tool for hosting or running a parenting course, please enquire through my website.

"What I gained from the course based on the material from Parenting for Life was invaluable, in particular the way I now understand and relate to my children more positively on a daily basis and using consequences to guide them has made me feel empowered as a parent."

Website www.thecourageousmumma.com

Thanks to...

Ella Leighton | DESIGNER & ILLUSTRATOR

Ella designs bespoke photo books and text-based books.
Photo Books: using her clients' photos, whether that's holiday, travel, family, wedding, memory or year books, she will use your photos to design books so personal to you, without the hassle of doing it yourself.
Text-based books: Ella has a degree in book art and design and has worked in publishing and collaborates with authors from concept through to publication.

She has a passion for illustration and her books and photo books are often accompanied by illustrations personal to the client, similar to the small scenes and characters throughout this book that bring the text to life. She has an eye for detail and simplicity throughout her work.

"I've known since a young age that I wanted to be in the design field. I love independent art films and I get inspired visiting great art galleries. The city, especially London, is like home to me, filled with life and soul. However, I am a country girl at heart! I am also a fanatic baker who is always looking for tasters!"

Website: *ellasbooks.co.uk* Instagram @ellas_books

Contributing photographers: James Baldwin, Thiargo Cerqueira, Edward Cisneros, Benjamin Combs, Irene Davila, Priscilla du Preez, Kai Dorner, Jon Flobrant, Janko Ferlic, Elena Ferrer, Joseph Gonzalez, Tim Gouw, Thomas Hareneth, Kasturi, Sebastian Leon Prado, Kelly Sikkema, Arno Smit, Annie Spratt, Allen Taylor, Brigitte Tohm, Pan Xiaozhen

- **Con,** for your endless generosity, patience and encouragement and love. You nutter for marrying me. Έγινα αυτό που είμαι επειδή με αγάπησες
- **Henry, Amelia, Tom, Charlie, Johnnie,** for sharing your hearts, keeping us laughing, for allowing Dad and I to influence you and for growing us. May our ceiling be your floor.
- **Yia Yia,** for believing in me.
- **Ella,** for taking a manuscript and making it beautiful; you are off-the-chart amazing.
- **Jo,** you are a gift. With your light-hearted joy, you have walked with me through the minefield of edits and crises of confidence, with the valuable balance of integrity and encouragement.
- **Advisors: Abi, Emma, Cat, Tara,** for your priceless advice, generous input and support.
- **Gardeners,** particularly Morag, Marianne and Ros. Thank you for the beauty and your vision.
- **Clients/Parents,** for trusting me and sharing your stories.
- **Caroline,** for your insight and dedication – and partnering with me.
- **My parents, siblings & friends,** you have shared, supported, advised, prayed, encouraged, loved, gifted, empowered, cautioned, honed, believed and inspired. You know who you are.

Nikki Sheffield | PHOTOGRAPHER

Being able to capture a moment lost in time is something so special to me. My main aim is to freeze these amazing moments and memories for others to cherish.
Website nikkisheffieldphotography.co.uk Instagram @nikki_sheffield_photography

Laura Eperjesi | PHOTOGRAPHER

My philosophy is simple, "real life is worth capturing". No false smiles or pretend studio shots. My work has won me awards with the British Institute of Professional Photography. Website lauraeperjesi.co.uk Instagram @lauraeperjesi

Amelia Purdy | PHOTOGRAPHER

Amelia lives in Toronto and has been a lifestyle photographer for almost ten years, focusing on families and weddings. She loves capturing real moments and documenting life as it is - mess and all! Website youbymia.ca Instagram @youbymia

Natalie Bedford | PHOTOGRAPHER

Natalie is an artist and the camera is one of her tools. Her eye for composition, texture and colour create stunning images of her favourite photographic subject: childhood. Website bynatalie.co.uk Instagram @bynatalieart

Index

Dear Parent,

Thank you for journeying this book with me.

There is no greater, tougher, more rewarding job in all the world than parenting.

Throughout my years of supporting and encouraging parents, I've never met one who doesn't want the very best for their child. Every mum or dad brings something unique and admirable to parenting. I love to see their tenacity, their depth of love and their desire to overcome the obstacles in family life. I'm still learning so much from the variety of parents I meet.

Whatever circumstances you are parenting in, there will be good days and challenging days: days when you feel you've got it all together and days when you feel you're the only one who hasn't - you're not alone on days like that!

You are amazing, don't ever think you're anything less.

Mads x